NOTIONS OF LIFE IN DEATH AND DYING

NOTIONS OF LIFE IN DEATH AND DYING

The Dead in Tribal Middle India

EVA REICHEL

MANOHAR
2009

First published 2009

ISBN 978-81-7304-823-4

Published by

Ajay Kumar Jain *for*
Manohar Publishers & Distributors
4753/23 Ansari Road, Daryaganj
New Delhi 110 002

Typeset at

Digigrafics
New Delhi 110 049

Printed at

Salasar Imaging Systems
Delhi 110 035

Contents

Prologue

MANBIR, MAYURBHANJ, NORTHERN ORISSA, INDIA
22 FEBRUARY 2006, 3.30 a.m.[1]

DEATH AT OUR NEIGHBOUR'S HOUSE: *NANA BURI*[2] DIES

Death has come close. At about 3.30 a.m. we hear the sudden and loud wailing of our neighbour, a widow living next door together with her four children. Her husband died the previous year and now her mother-in-law has died.[3] It is the same kind of

[1]The first part of the prologue is based on field notes which I took during my fieldwork among the Ho, a tribal community in Middle India, from December 2005 to April 2006. I was accompanied by my husband. We stayed in Manbir, a village on a plateau in the Jamda area of Mayurbhanj. This is the district in the north-eastern part of Orissa, the state close to Jharkhand, from which it is here separated by the river Balisudra. Manbir has about 400 inhabitants of whom more than half are Ho, in administrative terms a Scheduled Tribe (ST). Our neighbours belonged to the category 'General', a term they use to refer to themselves and by which they are referred to by others.

The issue of administrative categories will be discussed in Chapter Two.

[2]'*nana:* grandmother (paternal or maternal, sometimes used as vocative, also *jiyan*)'; '*buri*: old'. Both words are dictionary entries in John Deeney (2005: 261, 54). *Nana buri* is both address term and reference term.

[3]The information given to me was that *abuwa: nana buri* or 'our grandmother (had died)'.

If in a conversation three and more people are involved there are ways in Ho to indicate whether the person that one talks to is meant to be included in what is said or not. This is done by two different possessive pronouns to express 'our': (1) *aleya:* is the first person plural that excludes the person addressed, (2) *abuwa:* is the first person plural that includes the person addressed. So in this case I was included in the web of social relations.

wailing that by now is familiar to me in the Ho way of mourning their dead: a standardized arrangement of minims, crotchets and quavers within the range of a fourth, a set intonation and rhythm repeated again and again. A small kerosene lamp is lit. Within minutes villagers arrive: men, women, and children. As they set foot inside the courtyard the women—in the blink of an eye—start their ritual wailing, holding their arms crossed behind their heads. After paying a brief visit to the dead woman lying in her room, the male villagers squat down along the *pindigi*[4] talking to each other or just watching. After having left the room of the deceased the women stop wailing—as sudden as they had started it—and assemble in a corner of the courtyard. Our neighbour is one among the many involved and concerned. Men and women remain separate from each other. Children run around, playing, laughing. Whenever a female newcomer arrives the wailing starts afresh and is immediately answered by the wailing of our neighbour. Of the entire Ho community of Manbir I can only make out one more neighbour, an elderly Ho widow and her son, standing and watching, eye-witnesses to the scene, but not participating actively.

At 11 a.m. the cot with *nana buri* on it is taken out of her room and placed in the courtyard, her head pointing south.[5] By now the yard is quite crowded. The villagers gather around the cot at once. The wailing is resumed, this time very loud and including the children, girls and boys alike.[6]

That day the community well is only randomly used. Usually it is a very busy place. Is this a coincidence? A number of obligatory death rituals and ceremonies will follow in the days,

[4]*pindigi*: a small veranda-type elevation built around or in front of a Ho house.

[5]Ho usually sleep their heads pointing east. As soon as someone has died, the cot is moved around so that the head is in a southward direction, the feet to the north. This is also the position of the body inside the grave.

[6]It took several hours and elaborate procedures for the rubbing of the body with oil and turmeric and covering it with a newly bought white cloth, until it was eventually buried outside the village boundaries the very same day. To get to the burial site of the 'General' the funeral party (consisting of males only,) crossed the river Balisudra seven times.

weeks, and months to come. The *diri dulsunum*[7] rite is fixed for 3 March, the ninth day after (the physical) death.

BERLIN, GERMANY
10 JUNE 2006

DEATH IN MY FAMILY: MY BROTHER-IN-LAW DIES

There is a telephone call and a letter announcing his death and funeral. To better cope with the situation the shocked widow asks everyone to respect the privacy of the situation and her inability to communicate for the time being. At the funeral this poem by Ingeborg Bachmann[8] is read out:

'ich'.
[. . .]
Sklaverei ertrag ich nicht
Ich bin immer ich
Will mich irgendetwas beugen
Lieber breche ich.
Kommt des Schicksals Härte
Oder Menschenmacht
Hier, so bin ich und so bleib ich
Und so bleib ich bis zur letzten Kraft.
Darum bin ich stets nur eines
Ich bin immer ich
Steige ich, so steig ich hoch
Falle ich, so fall ich ganz.[9]

[7]'Pouring oil on the (burial) stone': part of the Ho mortuary rites. Cf. Chapter Five.

[8]German poetess, 1926–73.

[9]In: Bachmann, Ingeborg (2005: 11). As there was no English version of the poem available, I will attempt one myself:

'I'. Slavery I will not tolerate/ I am I—eternally/ I would rather break/ Than give in to no matter what./ Facing fate/ Facing men/ Here, such am I and such I'll stay/ I'll stay like this until my final breath./ So always will I be just this/ I am I—eternally/ In case I rise I will rise high/ In case I fall I will fall deep.

ONE

Introduction

Death and dying affect the living in a number of known and familiar ways. However, the responses to an actual death will be affected by the notions of life and death in the minds of those living on. But is death and dying not a very personal and intimate affair, an event, an event that arouses intense emotions such as grief, shock, despair, anger—emotions that make people feel sad, insecure, awkward, lost, and helpless? Do people faced with death not react spontaneously, more or less equally, worldwide? Is it not our heart that is the protagonist in this drama, directing the individual actors what to feel, what to do, how to cope? Are not emotions and 'our heart' true universals? So, if there was anything to analyse would it not be a matter of psychology rather than of sociology or anthropology?

Not so, argued Robert Hertz a hundred years ago in his seminal work on secondary burials (Hertz 1960[1907]). We believe that we react spontaneously, 'naturally', but in fact our behaviour is culturally shaped and so are our ideas and conceptualizations of death. Referring to non-western societies he points out that 'death has not always been [. . .] *felt* [my emphasis] as it is in our society' (ibid.: 28). The heart is not in control of the stage directions at the time of death, it is not even aware of them. The assumption of emotions or inner states as universals has also been critically analysed by Rodney Needham as the 'prejudice . . . that human nature is essentially the same everywhere' (Needham 1981: 67). In the same vein, Renato Rosaldo warns of 'the reckless attribution of one's own categories and experiences to members of another culture' (Rosaldo 1993: 171).[1]

[1]After Michelle Rosaldo fell to her accidental death while conducting fieldwork in the Philippines, R. Rosaldo, her husband, reflects on his

The thesis is that emotions are social constructs and that (death) rituals organize and orchestrate them (cf. Bloch, Maurice and Jonathan Parry 1982: 3; Piers Vitebsky 1993: 8; Nancy Scheper-Hughes 1992: 9). The thesis is also that people's behaviour revealed in the course of death rituals is normative and symbolic behaviour, which not only '"says" something, it also [. . .] "does" something' (Edmund R. Leach 1958: 147).

Physical death is as universal a phenomenon as is the empirical individual, member of the human species, who suffers it. The responses towards biological death, however, are not universally identical. They are never random reactions. They are meaningful, symbolic, and as such expressive. They differ from society to society. Huntington and Metcalf point out that 'the issue of death throws into relief the most important cultural values by which people live their lives' (Huntington and Metcalf 1979: 5). The stage director accounting for diverse and often complex cultural responses towards the 'organic event' is society and its central values (Hertz 1960: 27).[2] Thus the social expressions towards death and during mourning become culturally specific and cannot be considered independent of the particular social context. The values and norms of society will shape the convictions, beliefs and behaviour of the mourners in specific ways. As briefly outlined at the outset, in Middle India the death of an individual initiates a public process of elaborate social interaction beyond the narrow(er) boundaries of a particular household, displaying a clear script of well-structured, often standardized performances. In comparison, the Western concept of kinship is questioned. Here death is dealt with as a strictly personal and private affair involving as appropriate

---

emotions comparing them to a headhunter's rage at headhunting. On the one hand he admits that his emotional response to his wife's loss contributed immensely to his understanding of his informants' feelings and reactions, especially those of anger and rage. On the other hand and in hindsight he points out 'the discipline's methodological caution' against unwarranted identifications dictated by the anthropologist's common sense.

[2]Hertz's view of a personified society to which intentions and emotions are assigned in a rather rigid way was influenced by Emile Durkheim and has been criticized, e.g. by Bloch and Parry (1982: 4 ff); cf. Chapter Three.

dramatis personae usually a limited number of blood relations and friends, not knowing what to do or how to express their grief in culturally adequate ways beyond a formalized set of condolences. The lack of guidance from ritual is 'accompanied by a very considerable amount of maladaptive behaviour' (Vitebsky 1993: 236).[3] The funeral itself, commonly an affair of twenty to forty minutes, celebrates the individual(-istic) 'I'. 'I', focus and protagonist in the poem by Bachmann, refers to the individual as *the* central category and value of modern ideology, as Louis Dumont (1961, 1970[1966], 1986) would argue. An autonomous moral entity (bounded, unrelated, isolated, atomized, non-social, and free), this modern individual represents the supreme value in modern 'Western' society only.[4]

> The rational being . . . is peculiar to us, as is shown by the values of equality and liberty: it is an idea that we are having, the idea of an ideal. . . . In modern society . . . the Human Being is regarded as the indivisible, 'elementary' man, both a biological being and a thinking subject. (Dumont 1970[1966]: 9)

According to Dumont, this category is not universal as is the single biological human being. In 'non-modern societies' (Dumont 1986: 234)[5] the modern individual does not exist as a central category or value, since it is society itself that represents the supreme value as a whole. 'Non-modern' societies assume the unity of the cosmos and a universal order permeating the entire cosmos.[6]

[3]Vitebsky, whose monograph on the Sora of Orissa/Middle India will be discussed in Chapter Four, highlights this problem as well. He argues that on the whole 'the Sora funeral sequence does link public procedures and supposed inner feelings' (ibid.: 237).

[4]In Chapter Three the concept of the *person*, especially the *dividuum*, is discussed in more detail.

[5]The distinction between 'modern' and 'non-modern' societies is a sociological one. According to Dumont no value judgment is implied. In this sense 'non-modern societies' should not be misunderstood as pre-modern societies or as any other kind of disqualification. Both terms equally reflect ideological constructs. This is at least how Peter Berger explains the matter (1999: 129). Georg Pfeffer (2000a: 334), however, discusses Dumont's implicit evolutionism expressed in the terms 'modern', 'traditional', and 'non-modern'.

[6]Cf. Chapter Six.

Society as an integral part of the cosmos is consequently seen as governed by the same principles and subjected to the same 'natural' or global order of common values. Societies focusing on the cosmic-societal whole as the supreme value, and 'neglecting or subordinating the human individual', Dumont (1986: 279) calls holistic. The study of such societies should respect their respective wholenesses.

Georg Pfeffer argues that the symbolism expressed in death-related events and the relation between the living and the dead reveals central ideas about notions of life and afterlife prevailing in holistic societies: 'The loss due to death is often transformed into a state of fertility and enrichment.'[7] Do the tribal communities of Middle India see themselves as holistic societies 'based in the order of things, natural as well as social . . . copying or designing their very conventions after the principles of life and the world' (Dumont 1961: 36)? How is this being 'based in the order of things' articulated in the death-related 'conventions' in Middle India? With a change in perspective Margaret Trawick turns the sociological concept of holism into a value judgment, reading an additional meaning into it. 'One of our[8] most compelling dreams, one that we hold tightest to, is the dream of wholeness, the vision of a world whose meaning is contained within itself, of a life that is complete, of a place where all things touch' (Trawick 1992: xvii).

Is Middle India, then, with its tribal communities, such a 'place where all things touch'? What kind of an anthropological place is it?

My study is primarily one that utilizes the ethnographies of a limited number of tribal societies of the hilly and mountainous regions and plateaux of present-day Orissa and its neighbouring states, Chhattisgarh to the west and Jharkhand to the north (cf. Appendix 4: Mapping the Field). In five chapters it will focus from different angles on aspects related to death and dying and how this issue affects the relation between the living and the dead in culturally specific ways. Observations from my short

[7]Preface. In: P. Berger and R. Kottmann (2000: VI); my translation.
[8]Referring to herself and other Western anthropologists.

fieldwork of four months among the Ho of the Jamda area[9] will also be included, usually to contrast, illustrate, or complement what has been outlined in the monographs.

It was argued above that there is a relation between a particular kind of society and its specific cultural representations expressed e.g. during funeral rituals and in the normative behaviour of the mourners. As the ethnic categories of Middle India will throughout be referred to as tribal communities or, in a larger frame, as tribal societies, Chapter Two will take a brief look at the region and at the controversy about the term 'tribe' and the background of its having fallen into anthropological neglect for a considerable period of time. The notion of a tribal whole society will be outlined with respect to its values and ideas. Chapter Three will deal with the conceptualization(s) of death and dying as reflected in anthropological literature and the change of focus in the development of the discipline. Western notions will be contrasted with those prevailing in holistic societies. It seems that a major portion of fundamentally different ways of constructing society culminates in the respective concepts of *the person*. For this reason Bloch and his ideas about the notion of the *dividuum* have been discussed. Also, the studies of death rituals by Hertz, Arnold van Gennep, Parry, and again

[9]I conducted fieldwork in and around *Manbir*, a village and *Jamda*, a market town or *hato*, sites where the *Bage* clan or *kili* is the dominant clan (cf. Deeney 2002: 136), since they are said to have been the original settlers. The village priests or *diuri* of Manbir and Jamda are members of the Bage *kili*. Our assistant was Gurucharan Hansda (for names of Santal clan categories cf. Michael Yorke 1976), a Santal from Tarana. His wife is *kimin* (younger brother's wife) to Chumburu Purty, the Ho village headman or *munda* living in *Pathan Sai*. I was offered a namesake or *saki* relationship by his wife Santi, an act by which my husband became Ch. Purty's *saki*. After that we addressed each other exclusively by the term *saki*. Purty's ancestors, whom he addresses by name in rituals or *bongas* at the family level, are given in Appendix 3 as an example of the Ho institution of 'people of one cooking pot' or *miyad mandi chaturenko* (cf. Deeney 2005: 242; Deeney n.d.; Yorke 1976; Chapter Five).

The information that I gained in the course of participant observation will have to be checked in future fieldwork. In this study it is not discussed at length for this reason.

Bloch have been taken into consideration. What they have to say on the unity and continuity of life, death, and the afterlife, on responses to death, on the ceremonious treatment of the soul, and on the social obligations involved in this as well as on the structure of the death rituals as rites of passage proves to be important for the interpretation of death-related matters in Middle India.

All that is discussed in Chapters One, Two and Three is meant to serve as a background or thread guiding the reader through the maze of cultural diversities met in the ethnographic literature, to be examined in Chapters Four and Five. Fieldwork-based monographs have been chosen dealing with the Hill Juang of western Keonjhar (Charles McDougal 1963), the Sora of eastern Middle India (Vitebsky 1993), the Muria Gond of Bastar (Simeran M.S. Gell 1992), the Koya or Bison Horn Maria of southern Orissa (Ulrich Demmer 2007), and the Ho of Singhbum (Yorke 1976, Deeney n.d. et al.). What do these anthropologists, all of whom represent different 'schools' and probably carry distinctive preferences for different subject matters in their field luggage, reveal about the issue of death and relations between the living and the dead? Does the meaning that is attributed to death and dying by the indigenous people of Middle India pervade everything, so that it may be detected in the ethnographic material irrespective of and even despite the authors' theoretical outlook and focus ? In the final chapter a synopsis is given in a sort of bird's-eye view, preliminary rather than conclusive, of the main areas touched upon in this study.

TWO

The Issue of the Tribe in Middle India

Is a tribe an ethnic category? An ethnic group? An ideal type? A rural community? A group of backward Hindus? An imperfectly integrated class of Hindu society? A non-existing category? A whole society? A partial society? A politico-economic entity? The remainder of some primary stage of human development? A large, resistant society? A social construct? An empirical formation? An analytical tool? A coherent or autonomous group? A problem? An illusion?

Different notions resulting in different definitions: the number of the above question marks reflects the depth of the controversy, because all of the above 'statements' have been put forward in the debate of the issue of tribe. This chapter attempts an introduction to the debate.

The issues of 'tribe' and 'Primitive Society' have constituted the major field in anthropology since the beginning of the discipline. It is because of the kind of anthropological representation and the ethnographers' perspectives revealed in it, whether evolutionist, colonialist, functionalist, or structuralist, that the notion of tribe has become one of the most controversial in anthropology. Frederick G. Bailey remarked already in 1960 that, 'If "caste" is an emotive word, "tribe and caste" are doubly emotive. The debates about "the tribal problem" have moved scholars to unscholarly anger.' (Bailey 1960: 263)

To begin with, the terms 'tribe' or 'tribal' are disputed due to 'the stereotyped picture [. . .] and the associative meanings surrounding the words' (Gell 1992: 6) such as economic and educational backwardness, poverty, alcoholism, and promiscuity on the one hand as well as romanticized notions of tribal people being innocent, naïve, or somehow still (!) closer to nature on the other hand.[1] A patronizing stance on tribal society and culture[2] is formulated by the Indian government and published free of any kind of the self-consciousness prevailing in the Western anthropological debate. Biased opinions and derogatory comments dominating the official political discourse on tribals in India basically aim at modernizing and uplifting those 'down-trodden people'—despite the fact that the very members of the disputed category seem to be extremely proud of their status as members of a tribe. Is it because of these extremes that anthropologists have taken to euphemistic reformulations like 'ethnic groups', 'rural communities', or to dropping the subject altogether?

According to the Census of India 2001 more than 84 million people[3] belong to the category of Scheduled Tribes (ST)[4] and more than 166 million people to that of Scheduled Castes (SC). For the category of Other Backward Classes (OBC) no figures were found. These administrative categories are anchored in the Indian Constitution and result in a so-called 'protective discrimination'. The official politico-administrative terms and the anthropological understandings of these terms hardly coincide. This further complicates the debate.

[1]These polarizing images of tribal people are the result of a particular kind of classification and social construction which has in a different context convincingly been criticized by Edward Said in *Knowing the Oriental* (Said 1978: 31–49). Said analyses the process and effect of the anthropologist's projection of her/his view of man and the world onto 'the Orient' and its 'inhabitants'. According to Said, this kind of ethnographic representation reveals a lot about the anthropologist and her/his specific cultural background and very little about the society under research.

[2]Cf. ncw.nic.in/pdf reports/gender%/20profile-Jharkhand.pdf.

[3]The precise figures are 84 326 240 people registered as ST (8.2%), and 166 635 700 people (16.2%) registered as SC (Census of India 2001: T00-005).

[4]About 622 groups have been listed in an appendix or 'Schedule' of the Indian Constitution as Scheduled Tribes. The percentage of tribal communities and Hindu population differs greatly not only from state to state, but also within the states. So the overall tribal population of Orissa, i.e. officially 62 different tribes, roughly equals 22 per cent with more than 60 per cent living in the north and north-west of Orissa.

Also, the very usage of the term 'Scheduled Tribe' is controversial, as it is itself highly influenced by colonial ethnography[5] as pointed out by Roland Hardenberg (2005: 52) and Vitebsky (1993: 24). Moreover, the administrative categories seem to have been rather randomly imposed on certain communities, since 'the boundaries of tribal units never coincide with provincial borders' (Pfeffer 2002b: 211).[6]

'Tribe' is not an indigenous term. Members of a tribe usually refer to their own category as 'man' or 'humans' that way implying that they constitute *all* of mankind, *all* of humanity. As a matter of consequence everybody outside that particular tribal category is constructed as 'non-human', as remaining outside the tribe's moral order, as the 'other'. Nowadays indigenous people refer to themselves also as *adivasi* or as tribals. Although multilingualism is a characteristic of tribal communities, substantialist criteria of membership used to define tribes as bounded entities based on (a common) language, (a joint) territory, and political organization/autonomy, an assumption that does not correspond to the realities on the ground. This essentializing has been refuted by Pfeffer (2000b: 10–13, 2002a)[7] et al.

Until the 1950s the discussion of tribal affairs especially in Africa and the Americas, had figured prominently in anthropology, but eventually fell victim to the disregard of post-modern discourse. Somehow, however, the discourse on tribes had left out India until Independence, and after 1947 the focus of social anthropology was on caste. However specific, scientific, and controversial the notions of 'tribe' were that had been put forward

[5]*The Birhors: A Little Known Jungle Tribe of Chota Nagpur* (S.C. Roy 1925), *The Kharias* (S.C. Roy 1937), and *The Baiga* (Verrier Elwin 1939): these three examples, arbitrarily chosen among many more, imply that there are clear-cut and homogeneous cultural or social units, separate from and independent of each other.

[6]Cf. the discussion of the border between Jharkhand and Orissa in Chapter Five.

[7]Here also the theoretical positions that have played a role in the debate of the notion are discussed and criticized in detail. In his assessment Pfeffer refers to Boas (1911), Leach (1954), and Sahlins (1968); to Redfield (1947), Fried (1966), Gluckman (1960), Southall (1970), and Kuper (1988).

in the history of the anthropological debate, basic characteristics of tribal societies and tribal ideas have still been either ignored[8] or academically discriminated against.[9]

In the second half of the twentieth century the whole concept of 'tribe' began to be criticized as an 'illusion' (Southall 1970: 28) or an 'invention' (Kuper 1988). According to the latter, for instance, although anthropological understandings and models of primitive societies have constantly transformed, ever since the early days of evolutionism they have remained constructions and as such 'merely mirror images of ourselves' (Hardenberg 2005: 56).

Why, then, another effort to study, analyse, and compare the cultures of these categories or some of their central aspects? Is it anthropologically possible and meaningful to still employ the category of tribe? Is it still worthwhile focusing in one's fieldwork and modern theoretical effort on the construct of a tribal culture area? Or does this 'stage reveal nothing' (Fried 1966: 539)?

I neither want to repeat what can be read elsewhere nor give an overall summary of the debate and its critique. This has already efficiently been done by Uwe Skoda (2005: 49–60),[10] Hardenberg (2005: 52–70),[11] and Berger (2007: 55–8),[12] members of the Orissa Research Scheme, a project of the Free University of Berlin financed by the German Research Council

[8]Dumont who had so much to say on the unity of India and the issue of value-ideas spoke of 'only those primitive reserves' (see Pfeffer 1997: 5), paying little attention to tribal constructs of ritual purity.

[9]Although Verrier Elwin considered himself a philanthropologist, his representation of Hindu immigrants is criticized as 'one of the most obvious cases of academic discrimination' (Hardenberg 2005: 53).

[10]Skoda focuses on the controversies between Elwin and Ghurye in the 1940s and between Dumont/Pocock and Bailey in the 1950s and 1960s (Skoda 2005: 52 ff). He enlarges on the controversy also in Adivasi. Südasien.info (Skoda 2004).

[11]Hardenberg refers to the category of 'tribe' as an analytical model and uses it in inverted commas throughout his thesis. He applies it to the tribal society of the Niamgiri hills, where he did fieldwork.

[12]Berger makes the point that a general typology of the category is of secondary importance since in the actual fieldwork 'ethnographic descriptions of the specific social configurations should be paid attention to first' (Berger 2007: 57).

(DFG). They have conducted fieldwork on the social relations and society in different parts of Orissa/India among a number of tribal communities such as the Aghria, Dongria, Gadaba, and Rona.[13] These anthropologists' recent publications are based on essential characteristics of the concept of the tribe and tribal ideas, which will be outlined below. The hope is to gain some understanding of whether and how this concept is valid and alive in the Middle Indian context. Moreover, it will serve as a theoretical framework within which the ethnographic literature will be discussed (Chapter Four).

TRIBAL SOCIETY IN MIDDLE INDIA: IDEAS AND VALUES

Ethnographic description, analysis, and comparison of tribal societies in Middle India and elsewhere have been the focus of Pfeffer's work since 1982. Pfeffer suggests to employ the category 'tribal society' rather than 'tribes', since the administratively effected borders between allegedly distinct ethnic entities do not respect the social and cultural interdependence of and within tribal communities as well as their cultural complexity. This is more than a change of label. The term 'tribal society' is meant to include *all native inhabitants of the hilly regions*. Members of the Scheduled Tribes (ST), the Scheduled Castes (SC), as well as the Other Backward Classes (OBC) constitute a kind of 'permanent symbiosis'. However, ST and OBC as landowners (as patrons ritually superior and materially dependent) are opposed to SC as petty traders, cattle herders, craftsmen (as clients ritually inferior, often materially superior) (Pfeffer 2002b: 11, 1997: 7; Skoda 2005: 67).

The 'multiplex structure' (Pfeffer 2000b: 10) has already been pointed out by Marshall Sahlins (1968) as a significant criterion when discussing tribal society as being markedly different from hunting and gathering bands as well as from peasants. Besides, Dumont referred to tribes as whole societies contrasting them

[13]Tina Otten (2006) has worked on healing systems among the Rona. She does not refer to the controversy and consequently avoids making use of terms such as 'tribes' or 'tribal affairs'. She speaks of 'ethnic groups' instead.

with the categories of peasants, castes, or bands considered to be *part* of a whole society or an inclusive state (Dumont 1962: 120).[14]

Especially Sahlins figures prominently in Pfeffer's line of argument as well as in that of other anthropologists concentrating on that particular issue in that culture area in India. *Tribesmen* (Sahlins 1968), written within a neo-evolutionist framework, is a treasure trove of basic and topical insights into the complex world of the tribe.[15] In this Sahlins explains that the

> 'tribe' is . . . a body of people of common derivation and custom, in possession and control of their own extensive territory . . . a tribe is specifically unlike a modern nation in that its several communities are not united under a sovereign governing authority, nor are the boundaries of the whole thus clearly and politically determined. The tribe builds itself up from within, the smaller community segments joined in groups of higher order, yet just where it becomes greatest the structure becomes weakest: . . . Its economics, its politics, its religion are conducted . . . coincidentally by the same kinship and local groups: the lineage and clan segments, the households and villages . . . appear in charge of the entire social life. (Sahlins 1968: vii-viii)

In his model of a 'generalized tribal design' Sahlins characterizes a tribal society as a segmentary system whose levels of organization he identifies within 'a pyramid of social groups' or 'segmentary hierarchy' (ibid.: 15-16). He also offers a concentric model of social relations with the tribe at the periphery and the household in the centre surrounded by inclusive spheres of lineage kinsmen, of village relations, and of the broader relations of the tribal and inter-tribal sectors. Cohesion and social interaction is strongest in a tribe's smallest units: homestead and lineage, and weakest in the encompassing tribal whole.

Another important feature is the absence or distance of a

[14]For a discussion of principal differences of *partial* and *whole* societies, viz., peasants, bands, castes, and tribes cf. Sahlins (1968); Pfeffer (2002c: 10–11). These differences cannot be pursued here, but are important because they highlight the relation between the mode of production, the system of social organization (or its absence), and prevailing values.

[15]It is a book 'small in size but far-reaching in content' (Pfeffer unpubl.: 1; here also Sahlins' models are critically reconsidered in their applicability to the tribal conditions of Middle India).

state apparatus and government and the lack of administrative or political executive powers, specialized institutions of law and order. This results in a latent state of 'warre',[16] a tribe's 'normal state of disunity' (ibid.: 21). How then can relative peace be achieved, as 'the issue is peace' (ibid.: 9) and 'peacemaking is the wisdom of tribal institutions' (ibid.: 8)? Sahlins stresses the significance of kinship[17] and exchange in this respect. To characterize the functioning within a tribe Sahlins points to the lack of independent institutions. Politics, religion, economics are not 'so much different institutions as they are different functions of the same institutions. . . . The tribal structure is generalized' (ibid.: 15). The household is the smallest political entity and the major multivalent, functionally integrated socio-cultural institution. Economic cooperation and gift-exchange serve as peace-keeping measures. Sahlins defines the tribe *socially,* but characterizes his model as basically a moral plan, an 'organization of culture' (ibid.: 16) or a 'cultural formation at once structurally decentralized and functionally generalized' (ibid.: viii). As tribes are kin-based, the morality involved is kinship morality. The social sectors from household towards tribe in the concentric model or moral plan are 'so many steps of diminishing oneness' (ibid.: 19).

Reconsidering Sahlins' *Tribesmen,* Pfeffer (unpubl.) claims that his model of the 'levels of organization . . . and sectors of social relations do apply to tribal India', whereas he is critical of applying the African segmentary lineage system neatly in Orissa, 'there being no lineages in the African sense, but only "local lines" at the village level' (ibid.: 8) and beyond and above clans and tribes. Pedigrees of the Nuer type would not be in use[18] and ancestors would be forgotten, two aspects to be considered later in this study when discussing death rituals.

[16]Both Sahlins (1968: 5) and Pfeffer (2002c: 11) refer to Hobbes (*Leviathan*, part I, Chapter XIII) to illustrate that peace-keeping in tribal societies is never institutionally guaranteed.

[17]'Where peace is necessary or desirable, kinship is *extended* (my emphasis) to effect it' (Sahlins 1968: 11) pointing to the logic of expandability of classificatory kinship (categories).

[18]For more differences between Middle Indian tribal society and the 'African' and 'Biblical' model of a tribe cf. Pfeffer (2000 a: 338 ff).

There is a hierarchical system, Pfeffer says, of cultural values, in which the idea of hierarchy is expressed within the framework of a 'permanent order of relative seniority' (Pfeffer 2000b: 22) and affinal or kinship relations. This system of value-ideas in which a superior status is attributed to senior intra- as well as inter-tribal categories, prevails in Middle India, operating on the three structural levels of local lines, clans, and tribes. At all these levels a senior status is distinguished from a junior status, as neither any two groups nor any two empirical beings share the same status. Senior status, however, neither implies degradation or exploitation of the junior status, nor does it constitute a means of political or economic dominance. Since the system of hierarchy is supposed to pervade everything and is expressed in separate cooking sites, rules of commensality, marital rules, etc., all of the cultural transactions of life, including after-life, are touched. This system is shared by the patrons and clients of the tribal societies[19] thus transcending officially drawn borderlines artificially separating categories such as the SC and OBC from the ST. It constitutes a model or societal order, almost one that Lévi-Strauss characterizes as 'cold',[20] not because of the small size of the tribal population, but because of its 'small-*scale* (emphasis: original) order ruled by face-to-face relationships' (Pfeffer 2000b: 23). True, there are processes of transition, transformation, and history, and they have always taken place, since tribal societies have never existed in isolation. Beyond the value of seniority basic concepts of marriage, death, and religion are shared by these categories, however regionally different, depending on the specific social and ideological configuration of the groups involved. For this reason the notion of a 'tribal society' in singular and plural has been suggested including those classified by the government as 'Untouchables' (SC) and 'Backward Classes' (OBC) as mutually dependent in terms of their social and cultural identity.

[19]Trade, contact with the outer world and a number of necessary activities are considered polluting and thus to be performed by clients (members of the SC) of 'junior' status.

[20]The reference to Lévi-Strauss's notion of a 'cold' society is explained in Pfeffer (2000b: 23, 26; 2002a: 16).

Pfeffer combines the issue of seniority with the concept of purity/impurity and matters sacral and secular to the effect that at the highest level certain tribes are senior to junior tribes (e.g. Ho[21]–Munda, Gadaba–Bondo, Bhuiya–Juang[22]). At the household level, an elder brother is senior to his younger brother. At the village level the village priest is senior to the secular village headman, etc. All of this is against the assumption of tribal egalitarianism and has been discussed time and again.

This 'collectivity' of ideas is constitutive of the tribal society of Middle India. It links (sacral/secular/immaterial) status and seniority irrespective of wealth and power, (relative) purity and pollution, *and* their being related to a 'transcendent existence', an implied greater 'proximity to the world beyond', the 'total submission to transcendent forces', and 'outerworldly devotion' (Pfeffer 2000a: 342–4). Accordingly, Pfeffer suggests *otherworldliness* as the ultimate value, following the indigenous logic of the hierarchy of highly differentiated status assignments.

Tribal society can be seen as holistic; it is a society that can do without systematic and despite occasional, in any case poor and distant state performance. 'The order of things'[23] is a network of affinity and descent resulting in gift-exchange, kin-based tribes as large, non-bureaucratic, supra-locally organized units of reference. The 'place where all things touch'[24] seems to be an ideological or mental one, a realm, where supra-individual value-ideas such as hierarchy, seniority, purity, status, kinship, affinity, otherworldliness etc., are interrelated and dominant. All of these rank—as a matter of principle—superior to matters of wealth and power: two individuals may be equally poor but of different status.

How are the a.m. value-ideas related to notions of death and dying in the tribal whole societies of Middle India? Anthropological literature on this issue will be examined next before taking a closer look at how this topic is dealt with in the ethnography of Middle India.

'A dream of wholeness, a vision of a world that is complete'

[21]Cf. Chapter Five.
[22]Cf. Chapter Four.
[23]Cf. Dumont (1961) quoted in Chapter One.
[24]Cf. Trawick (1992) quoted in Chapter One.

(Trawick 1992) was quoted in the Introduction as a guideline for analysis. Following the discussion in this chapter, the 'statement' will be complemented by others such as 'oneness',[25] 'tribal wisdom',[26] and 'otherworldly devotion'.[27]

[25]Sahlins 1968, when discussing the advance from the sector of a household to that of a tribe within his concentric model of social relations.

[26]Sahlins 1968 on the tribal praxis of peacemaking.

[27]Pfeffer (2000 a) on the implications of the principle of seniority.

THREE

Notions of Death and Dying

Western notions of death and dying effect a culturally specific obligation of mourning the dead. They affect the (common sense) understanding of the relation between the living, the dying, and the dead in decisive ways. Western construction(s) of death will be delineated here to serve as a blueprint and to more successfully grant access to a cultural logic that provides for accepted ritual and guidance illustrating what it means to conceive of death in ways fundamentally different.

WESTERN NOTIONS

References to the *moment* or the *hour* of death reflect a notion of death as a clearly recognizable (natural) event that usually occurs within a very brief period of time. This is the generally accepted Western conception of death. It depends on an individual's religious conviction whether s/he believes in 'life beyond death'. In terms of religion it is a matter of the separation of the soul from the body, and the context remains an individual one. Usually death is seen as the 'end of life'[1] implying that death and life are two utterly separate categories. There are clear distinctions between the point in time of physical death, the brief period 'in which the dead person is "laid out" for final rites and the corpse's immediate and definite being removed from the social context of the living' (Sally C. Humphreys 1980: 265). Legal and biomedical issues surround death, so a number of legal and medical specialists will probably be involved when it comes to

[1]This is the denotation given in the *Oxford Advanced Learner's Dictionary*: headword 'death', 2nd entry (1995: 287).

dying.[2] Because of the new possibilities of prolonging 'life' physiologically, death is being redefined neurologically in terms of an individual's brain function. Brain death can be precisely measured by sophisticated instruments in technologically well-equipped hospitals.[3] Due to the process of medicalization, the process of dying often becomes concealed within the hospital. Responsibilities may be handed over to medical professionals, and relatives distanced from the process of dying. In a society in which this is considered 'normal', the community as a whole will distance itself from the issue of death to the effect that many have never seen a corpse or 'only in the carefully stage-managed context of the funeral parlour, the body elaborately packaged and beautified' (ibid.). Shame, discomfort, and repulsion may become dominant, so much so that Antonius Robben speaks of the 'pornography of death' (Robben 2004: 4). It has been suggested that it is for such reasons that the anthropology of death is poor: 'ethnographers have been inhibited by their own taboos from studying it' (Humphreys 1980: 265).[4]

There is an anthropology of *death rituals*, however, which

[2]This is reflected in contemporary literature, film and theatre, and the subject seems to be of some public interest. *Whose Life is it Anyway?* by Brian Clark (1978), for example, is a British play dealing with legal and medical aspects of dying inside a hospital. According to Clark, much harder than working the literary theatre version into a script for a feature film was the rendering of the original into an American version complying with the American legal and medical *system of dying*. Also, translating from British into American English was not a technical or linguistic challenge in the first place, but Clark had to respect culturally specific ways of thinking and talking about notions of death and dying.

[3]The Western assumption of death as an event of one instant is betrayed as fiction, though, by the ongoing debates on active and passive euthanasia and the controversy about ways of dealing with processes of dying inside a hospital restricting medical care to technical care.

[4]This 'suppression thesis' has been contradicted, however, by Johannes Fabian (1973), whose essay will be discussed in this chapter.

Without hinting at any (speculative) explanation Richard Huntington and Peter Metcalf (1979: XIII) confirm 'three generations of silence', in which issues of death and mortality were not publicly discussed in American society.

deals primarily with cultural variations in non-Western societies. Its history will be outlined in the next chapter. Special attention will be paid to those who have offered cross-cultural studies, embedding the cultural issue of death in the social context of the respective societies.

NOTIONS OF DEATH AND DYING IN ANTHROPOLOGY

From the beginning of the academic discipline anthropologists have been interested in the 'exotic' other, such as tribes. As a result, exotic tribal customs such as their elaborate mortuary rites and death rituals have attracted their attention. These practices reveal tremendous variations and express divergent conceptualizations of *life* and death, of dying and mourning. Anthropological search for meaning should aim at going beyond the description of the customs and rituals as such and not conceive of these as self-contained units. The initial interest in the rituals, however, was guided by an interest in their *origins* and *evolution* rather than in finding out about particular '*form[s] of humanity*' (Dumont 1986: 205/206, emphasis original).

It is James Frazer (1890) who, by focusing on the ritual murder of the priestly king, reveals a relation between death and the act of killing on the one hand and the idea of fertility and regeneration on the other. One hundred years later this idea still plays an important role in the anthropological discourse on death. It also has been taken up by Bloch and Parry (1982).[5] When dealing with matters of death, Frazer's bias, however, was more with religion, as the subtitle to *The Golden Bough* suggests, and with people's beliefs about death and afterlife. Within the theoretical limitations of evolutionism, of the doctrine of survivals and diffusionism, 'religion' was interpreted as an early and overall erroneous attempt at science;[6] exotic customs and death rituals were seen as irrational practices reflecting 'wrong', primitive, or anachronistic beliefs—relics of and evidence for past 'crude' stages of mankind and past social forms.

[5]Cf. Chapter Three.

[6]The three stages of evolution as suggested by Frazer are 'magic–religion–science'.

With such attitudes prevailing in the late nineteenth and early twentieth century anthropology, the interpretation of ritual practices was exploited in order to prove preconceived ideas and convictions about 'the other', regularly depicted as less advanced, less rational, and less logical. The ethnographer's aim was not to make sense of past and present eras in cross-cultural studies of 'their common inhabitant, the social person' (Huntington and Metcalf 1979: 10) or to uncover a *constructive* view of the cultural possibilities and choices of *Anthropos*. This was before Malinowski's fieldwork methodology of participant observation and his focus on the 'native's point of view' became the generally accepted dogma of the discipline.[7]

Sociology and sociologists have also been attracted by the issue of death in terms of its social dimension. Emile Durkheim and Marcel Mauss, Robert Hertz and Arnold van Gennep have had a lasting influence by analysing events and processes within the social context of societal wholes. Durkheim, for example, had studied ethnographic material on the death rituals of Australian aborigines. He came to the conclusion that individual grief experienced at the death of another human being 'is expressed collectively in culturally prescribed ways of mourning'.[8] Although grief may be considered a universal emotion of bereavement, its social expression in mourning is culturally specific, a collective obligation. Already in his study of suicide Durkheim had argued that behaviour commonly considered profoundly individual, was in fact guided by (social) norms.

For the purpose of this book the studies of Hertz (1960[1907]) and van Gennep (1960[1909]) will be considered. It was not until the translation of this work into English in 1960 that they became influential in the anthropological discourse of death. Hertz, a scholar of Durkheim, had analysed processes of dying, especially secondary burials, in Borneo and in Polynesia. Van Gennep had examined the *structure* of death-related rituals cross-culturally and thus conveyed a fresh strategy of re-interpreting ethographic material on death.

[7]Malinowski's assumption that people take to religion because of man's universal fear of death has, however, been theoretically informed by functionalism and been discarded in the discourse of death by now.

[8]Quotation in Robben (2004: 7).

Elements of ceremonial behaviour were no longer the relics of former superstitious eras, but keys to a universal logic of human social life. . . . Rituals were analysed as dramatic representations of the function of 'separation'. Van Gennep's study proposed a radically different assessment of the meaning of ritual behaviour, one subversive of the entire project of ethnocentric evolutionism. (Huntington and Metcalf 1979: 11)

According to Robben, 'the anthropology of death led a rather dormant existence' (2004: 2) after the early writings and turned to the collection and ethnographic description of mortuary rituals. Bloch and Parry (1982) and Johannes Fabian (1973) basically share this assessment.

In his essay Fabian takes a critical look at the *status quo* of the discipline, its traditions, some of its main representatives (Tylor, Frazer, Boas, Hertz, Malinowski, Kroeber, Turner, Lévi-Strauss, and Geertz) and at their theoretical perspectives and loci of attention. Fabian identifies a tendency to see death as a self-contained experience[9] and a concentration on the customs of culturally different Others, a context-free way of dealing 'only with the purely ceremonial aspects of death' (Fabian 1973: 178). He criticizes this dilemma as a self-imposed 'folklorization, parochialization and exoticization' (ibid.). He calls for an 'anthropology of *death*' replacing the 'anthropology of *deaths*' in order to gain knowledge transcending local particularities. The paradigm of intersubjectivity needs to be implemented, he says, the construction of a 'social hermeneutic and an interpretation of social reality . . . which conceives of itself as part of the process it attempts to understand' (Fabian 1973: 201). That way the dichotomy between the ethnographic 'they' and the anthropologists' 'we' or 'us' may be bridged, and the focus from 'how others die' may shift to a reflection on 'how we die', paying respect to cultural differences, but not ignoring or excluding similarities.

R. Rosaldo, too, touches the problem of the person of the anthropologist as constitutive of the process of ethnographic

[9]For similar reasons R. Rosaldo criticizes this approach for not considering 'rituals as being linked with larger processes unfolding before and after the ritual period . . . the formal ritual is but a phase' (1993: 174).

representation. When referring to his informants' and his own experience of death, for example, he makes use of an image of two circles (of experience) that are 'partially overlaid, partially separate. They are never identical' (Rosaldo 1993: 171). So bridging the gulf between 'them' and 'us' is the idea, an overlapping rather than identification.

Likewise Vitebsky suggests that anthropological analysis is 'valid only to the extent that it can help us to reflect on our own mortality and our own feelings of love and anger, loss and continuity' (Vitebsky 1993: 8; Chapter Four). Differentiating the process of anthropological analysis further, Vitebsky discusses the notion of empathy and its implications, the issue of emotions in anthropological representation. Empathy, he argues, reaches the meanings and relationships of concepts beyond our understanding, and it is more than empathizing with a specific mental state of mind such as 'love' or 'anger'. In fact, he interprets empathy as a social category, for

> even at the distance of being a reader, this involvement is with other persons and implies a sense of time. In empathizing with others, we make an imaginative leap which involves seeing ourselves in another person's situation, a situation which represents a moment in a sequence. Thus I take feelings to be interpersonal and social as well as internal and private. (ibid.: 9)

The dimension of emotions, feelings, and empathy is either discussed controversially or avoided in anthropological theory, claiming feelings to be primarily something intrapersonal and thus the subject matter of psychology rather than anthropology,[10] a science concerned with interpersonal relations. According to Vitebsky, however, this need not necessarily be a contradiction if emotions are assumed to be social constructs. Empathizing with the feelings of others may be based on an 'awareness of a narrative of their interrelatedness as (social) persons' (ibid.).[11]

[10]Cf. Chapter One.

[11]It should be mentioned here that Vitebsky does not seem interested in a theoretical debate of these aspects. Neither is he advocating some kind of 'anthropology of emotions'. He tries to represent Sora (ways of)

The linguistic turn in anthropology is identified with Claude Lévi-Strauss. He had made the proposition that anthropology was, at base, the study of death. So it should be named *entropology* instead, a discipline studying the processes of disintegration (Lévi-Strauss 1970 [1955]: 367). And death, he said, was to be analysed as the 'core of a language, a universal code' (Fabian 1973: 195), a phoneme within the system of communication that is culture. In such a language-oriented approach, Fabian continues, anthropological study may turn to 'the search for the *specific* [original emphasis] message, the "what" that may be expressed in the language of death, . . . the "meaning" of culturally defined reactions to death' (ibid.).

What are these specific messages? How can they be found and studied? Do death rituals encapsulate 'a culture's wisdom' (Metcalf and Huntington 1979: 1), if understood as related to the societal whole? These issues have been explored by Hertz, van Gennep, Bloch, and Parry with reference to non-Western societies.

THE ANTHROPOLOGY OF DEATH IN HOLISTIC SOCIETIES

The comparative approaches of Hertz, van Gennep, Bloch, and Parry are important in the field of the cross-cultural analysis of death. Hertz's and van Gennep's structural approaches offer analytical tools that can be applied to every mortuary rite, in fact to an enormously wide range of rituals. In modern ethnographies, anthropologists keep employing these tools.[12]

---

managing their lives, and in this he deals with the 'Dialogues with the Dead' as a specific Sora kind of disentangling psychological and sociological levels and matters, personal as well as social.

[12]In his chapter on 'mortuary rituals' Robben (2004: 9ff) deals with Hertz, van Gennep, and Parry. He calls Hertz's study (1907) the 'single most influential text in the anthropology of death' (ibid.) and states that both, Hertz and van Gennep, may count on wide acceptance in anthropology since 'hardly anything as daring has been attempted since then' (ibid.: 13). In the same introduction Robben presents modern monographs related methodologically to Hertz's and van Gennep's

All these authors have studied holistic societies[13] in which death is seen as a social event, the starting point of a ceremonial process that has to deal with the complex entwinement and difficult separation of body, spirit or soul, and mourners. Irrespective of existing cultural variations, there tend to be structural elements and topics that can be uncovered and generalized. In all of these societies, death is considered an initiation into a social afterlife, a transition leading from one state to another. This moving ahead or 'up' at the time of death again is neither unique nor irreversible, but rather a structured passage comparable to other transitions during life such as birth, puberty, and marriage. All transitions are marked by a number of complex rituals displaying amazing similarities.

In this context Hertz, van Gennep, Bloch, and Parry focus on complementary aspects, adding to one another in a number of ways. Van Gennep draws from Hertz, who had published his analysis of secondary burials two years before. Bloch (1988) extends Hertz's stress on the processual aspects of the period *after* death to those of the whole period of life. He also analyses the notion of the *dividuum* in its implications for the discussion of life, death, and rebirth, a concept challenging our intellectual capacities of understanding the logic of other cultures. Bloch and Parry (1982) discuss the funerary symbolism of fertility and coincide with Hertz in their conclusion of a regeneration of life and a continuation of society.

In his interpretation of secondary burials, Hertz (1907) interprets mortuary rituals as a societal reaction[14] to death and a means of finally restoring social order. He interprets death not as an isolated incident involving the deceased physically and his

approaches. Also, Huntington and Metcalf (1979) understand their discussion of 'death' as an elaboration of certain aspects of the analysis offered by Hertz.

[13]Hertz's study (1960[1907]) is primarily about the funerary cults of the Malayo–Polynesian speaking peoples, especially the Dayak of Borneo/Indonesia. Hertz has not been 'in the field' himself, but did research mainly in the British Museum from 1904 to 1906. Bloch has done fieldwork among the Merina of Madagascar, and Parry in Banaras (Varanasi), India.

[14]In the sense of a non-individual, social response.

close relations emotionally. In the societies under study death is seen as an attack on the social order of the whole group and consequently the whole group must respond and will do so in different ways depending on their different ways of being affected. Hertz analyses the fate of the body of the deceased, of his soul, and of the mourners independent of each other, but also in their interrelatedness. He shows that these three distinct aspects express the same idea of transition[15] and are ritually taken care of in the mortuary rites resulting in a change of status according to a familiar and public pattern. 'Death is not originally conceived as a unique event without any analogue' (Hertz 1907: 81). The similarity of the purification rites, for example, in birth, marriage, and death betray a basic analogy. According to Hertz there is also an analogy between the body and the soul of the deceased and the condition of the mourners. In this, the development of the body serves as a model for the fate of the soul. The analogy also holds true for life's

> heterogeneous and well-defined phases, to each of which corresponds a more or less organized social class. Consequently each promotion of the individual implies the passage from one group to another: an exclusion, i.e. death, and a new integration, i.e. rebirth. . . . This transition from one group to another . . . always supposes a profound renewal of the individual which is marked by such customs as the acquisition of a new name, the changing of clothes or of the way of life. (ibid.: 80–1)

Hertz keeps coming back to the implications of Western individualism and the relevance of the Western notion of death as a sudden event, an ethnographic observation of some consequence. 'In our own society', he says, 'no interval separates the life ahead from the one that has just ceased' (ibid.: 28). In the societies that he studies, this interval is always there and sometimes a lengthy affair of several years. We believe that we are either alive or not alive, one thing or the other, as Bloch (1988: 11) puts it. But that belief, Bloch goes on, is not shared by many other cultures. Many peoples believe in an in-between period which Hertz calls the 'intermediary', van Gennep the

[15]Cf. E.E. Evans-Pritchard in 'Introduction' to Hertz (1960: 15).

'liminal', Victor Turner the 'betwixt and between', a period when the deceased is neither alive nor finally dead. They imagine death to be part of a long transformative process reflecting processual, cyclical or stage-like notions of death. In this process, when the soul is being ritually separated from the body, the dead person will still be conceived as remaining a part of society.

The interpretation of death as a social affair and a complex cultural pattern is no anthropological 'fiction'. The logic of the view is demonstrated by the fact that the ritual treatment in death rituals is restricted to social persons. When an uninitiated child dies, for example, it will not be ceremoniously taken care of as a socially mature person will.

In anthropological literature death as a process is often referred to as a long, risky, and dangerous journey, a metaphor also applied to the representation of life and indicating that death as a second journey is just a continuation of the first, not seldom differentiated in more detail than people's empirical world. But there is also the view that these are not two separate and consecutive processes: the journey of life itself is seen as a 'process of gradual dying' (Bloch 1988: 13). Thus what for Western people happens at the end of their lives, for others may begin rather early in life.

Van Gennep (1909) introduces a model of a tripartite structure underlying *all* rites of passage including death rituals. In his survey of death-rituals throughout the world van Gennep makes use of Hertz's analysis of secondary burials in Indonesia. The life crises or passages that an individual passes through in his lifetime become the focus of elaborate rituals that he calls 'rites of passage'. These rituals reveal three distinct phases: a preliminal phase of separation, a liminal one of transition, and the post-liminal one of reintegration. In the first phase the corpse is being disposed of temporarily. As death is considered polluting to those who are dealing with it, the mourners are separated from society and the daily routines of communal life. In the course of the liminal phase of transition, mourners must observe a number of taboos. The soul is supposed to remain close to the corpse. In analogy to the state of the corpse it is assumed to share its state of decay and to be in a deplorable and dangerous state itself. For this reason, in order to pacify the soul it has to be equipped with food, water, etc., on its long journey to the after-world of the ancestors. To his surprise van Gennep found that the rites of separation are relatively inconspicuous, whereas the rites of the second phase are the most elaborate. In the post-liminal phase the soul is integrated into the world of the dead, and the mourners are re-integrated into society. In a joint meal the final passage of the soul is celebrated collectively. The period of pollution and the culturally prescribed obligatory phase of mourning have come to an end. Social order and social purity are restored, when all of the three phases have been accompanied by the proper rituals.

Assessing Hertz's essay on the representation of death and drawing from his own fieldwork and other ethnographic material, *Bloch* (1988) discusses the topic of boundaries, more precisely the assumption of clear-cut boundaries between being dead and being alive. He confirms that for the Merina of Madagascar death is a stage in a drawn out process which begins long before the physical event and which will continue afterwards. By highlighting spirit possession as just one common example[16] he illustrates how in other cultures the boundary between being dead and being alive is not so clear. The spirit of a deceased is not invisible for good, but can empirically be perceived and heard through a medium.[17] The dead or his spirit obviously have not stopped participating in the lives of the living. Also, the transformation of turning into a medium is achieved by a process which is seen as similar to the process of dying, and the possessing of the medium's mind by the deceased's spirit is understood as an act of death on the part of the medium and as an act of (temporary) rebirth of the dead. Reversely, after the completion of the trance or spirit possession, the social person that had acted as the medium, will be re-born. So again our notion of death as a final termination, or something unique, is challenged. Dying may be a comparatively common experience

[16]Other examples are the journey of the spirit at the period of dreaming or during illnesses.

[17]Much of Vitebsky's ethnography (1993) is based on this experience. Cf. Chapter Four.

if death is seen as an intrinsic part of life, acted out in the various passages and ritual dramas of life.

The concept of the person or rather the concept of the *dividuum* has consequences for our understanding of death. Again, the issue is about boundaries. In our Western societies, Bloch points out, we conceive of a person primarily as an individual, a unit (separate from other equally functioning units) that consists of elements, material and immaterial, like soul, body, blood, flesh that are considered to be linked in an interrelated, inseparable, and unique way that is believed to be 'real'. The entity as such is the smallest unit which is complete in itself, and which cannot be subdivided or else the state of the unit would be endangered. In our view, Bloch continues, someone is considered dead when one of his/her constitutive elements, e.g. the heart stops beating or when the functioning of the brain has been decided to have come to an end. This intertwining of the parts *within* an individual is assessed as being of a primary order, whereas the individual's being linked to other individuals, for example, emotionally, morally, or socially is seen as relationships of a secondary order and of a different and inferior quality. In our logic, when an in-dividual dies, the whole person will die. Consequently our concept of the indivisibility of the individual creates a sharp boundary between life and death, reflecting an 'all or nothing understanding' (Bloch 1988: 13). So *one* burial will do.

In holistic societies the prevalent notion of the *dividuum* implies that elements which combine *within* a person can simultaneously combine externally and independently in 'cross-cutting wholes' (ibid.). There are no links of a primary or secondary order. The ontological status of the links between *dividuums* is assumed just as real as the constituent elements of the individual. This has tremendous consequences for the concept and meaning of death. Although in such a society an empirical individual will also be considered as having died at the 'time of death', those parts, however, will survive, as they are linked to the 'cross-cutting whole', which continues to exist in other individuals, groups, lineages, etc.—independent of the dying individual. So death is a loss, but it is not a total loss. When a person dies, only a part of it will die and decay materially, another part will continue to exist, and it will exist equally materially. Again, the boundaries are different from Western conceptualizations. Death is not conceived as an absolute category. Dying is turned into a transformative process of exchange between life and death, a continuous 'taking apart and putting together' (Bloch 1988: 17). Bloch exemplifies and summarizes this interpretation in the sentence: 'When a Southern Somali dies, his bone/lineage does not die' (ibid.).[18] Rephrased in positive terms: the lineage will continue to exist because of the deaths of its members. Fertility as a means of establishing existence and active continuity has been created out of death.

Consequently, metaphors of fertility, sexuality, and growth often dominate the symbolism in death rituals and draw attention to their being life-centred rather than death-centred. Bloch and Parry (1982) concentrate on this seeming paradox, interpreting its symbolism and meaning. Frazer's idea of fertility and Hertz's exploration of secondary burials are combined and exploited for their line of argument. Fertility is defined as a life value inherent in people and/or animals and/or crops. It is a category prevalent in nature, a metaphor and symbol of maturing, growing, and continuity. Bloch opposes (female, uncontrolled) sexuality, human reproduction, and *natural* fertility which are often associated with biological death to a sacred, non-sexual ancestral fecundity as a means of the reproduction of the controlled social order. In societies with a cyclical world-view death is part of a cyclical process of renewal. Death as a passage is a transition or birth into something new, its actors obtaining a new social identity. Once the polluting aspects of death have been dealt with, his/her social aspects require attention, those

[18]Bloch discusses here in some detail the concept of death as presented by Helander (1988).

The relation to what has been said before is as follows:

The 'Southern Somali' refers to the empirical being or individual, 'dies' refers to his biological death and the ongoing decomposition of the soft parts of the corpse, i.e. the flesh; 'bone/lineage' refers to the 'cross-cutting whole'; 'does not die' refers to the continuation of the social order, a *re-generation* of the *social* body with the bones demonstrating its permanence.

that society had 'grafted'[19] upon the individual turning him into a social person. This is being done in the course of the second burials. Bloch and Parry draw a dividing line between biological fertility symbolized in and associated with marriage rituals, and spiritual fertility celebrated in death rituals and resulting in the continuation of the group. As spiritual fertility reproduces society by regenerating and reasserting the supraindividual values of purity and permanence, it ranks superior to the biological processes of birth, reproduction, and death, all associated with unpredictability, lack of control, and social impurity. In the light of this interpretation, statements such as 'Life-giving Death'[20] begin to seem less paradoxical and become resolved. After the cessation of the process of physical decay, the soul, bones and spiritual essence are believed to live on in the world of the ancestors. There the soul is assumed to exist as a resource to be reborn implanting life-force and vitality into a baby. Thus the immortal soul of a *dead* person has *given life* to a new-born being. In case this being lives through the birth rites successfully (and does not die before the naming rituals) the biological being will be transformed into a (social) person achieving a social identity. It is due to this process that the social body of society becomes renewed, the gap filled, and order restored.

In the next chapter a number of ethnographies will be examined dealing with the tribal societies of the Juang, the Sora, the Muria, the Koya, and the Ho in Middle India. What importance is attributed to the issue of death? How is this social phenomenon interpreted? How are the ideas discussed so far reflected in the respective monographs, how do they deviate?

[19]This is a metaphor employed by Hertz (1960) when enlarging upon the difference between the biological and the socio-cultural being.

[20]This is the title of an essay by Daniel de Coppet (1981).

FOUR

Relations Between the Living and the Dead in Tribal Middle India

If in holistic societies death is integrally part of life and the dead are integrally linked to the living, the issue of death will lend itself particularly well to an analysis of monographs written by ethnographers adhering to different anthropological 'schools'.

The first monograph to be examined in this respect is one on the Hill Juang by Charles W. McDougal (1963).

THE HILL JUANG OF WESTERN KEONJHAR

From 1960 to 1962 C.W. McDougal did fieldwork for 15 months among the Hill Juang, a tribe of shifting cultivators[1] in the

[1]A word on shifting cultivation, slash-and-burn techniques, and swidden fields (McDougal 1963: 26 ff), since the ownership of land and the kind of its cultivation is an important factor in tribal society and in tribals' self-image.

The Hill Juang clear hill-slope fields by slash-and-burn techniques. These fields are referred to as swiddens. Swiddens may be cultivated for three years or so before clearing new fields. The technical term for this type of horticulture is shifting cultivation. So slash-and-burn cultivation, swidden cultivation, and shifting cultivation are almost synonymous. They would operate in alternating cycles. The soil in the swiddens may be hoed or in more recent times ploughed, since hoe cultivation presupposes the general availability of land which is no more given today. The transformation from hoe cultivation to adopting plough cultivation on permanent (private) property affects matters of inheritance, bridewealth, etc. That way it bears on the social fabric of a tribe and is more than an economic affair proper.

For a discussion of this complex combining economic questions and their social consequences cf. Pfeffer (2002d: 26ff, 61ff) and Sahlins (1968:

Keonjhar District of Orissa (cf. Appendix 4 for McDougal's site of fieldwork). 'The Social Structure of the Hill Juang' is the title of his dissertation, in which he aims at providing a detailed structural–functional analysis of Juang traditional society. There is the little explored, yet highly developed men's house system serving as a dormitory for young, unmarried boys and simultaneously as a community centre for grown-up males discussing village affairs.[2] There is also the particular age system, a 'structure which assigns both males and females to a series of groups based on age' (ibid.: 176) and status. On the whole age criteria rank prominently in the allocation of an individual's membership to a fixed age-set within her/his generational level, opposing her/him to other fixed age-sets. Within each generational level the principle of seniority is recognized. Supported by Juang kinship terminology, each of the opposing blocks contains alternating generations and excludes adjacent ones. Whole villages are classified in that way, not just individuals. Apart from the dualism of generation every Juang is set within a second dualism created by marriage: any village will be marked as belonging to either the marriageable *bondhu* category or the non-marriageable *kutumb* half. This division includes the Bhuiya in Keonjhar, who are considered the senior 'siblings' of the junior Juang.

McDougal displays an enormous wealth of information on and a systematic description and analysis of Juang society revealing its 'homogeneous and intricate social structure' (Pfeffer 2002d: 72). As he is primarily concerned with matters of

29). As for the general availability of land, Yorke claims that in the case of the Saranda Forest Area of Chhota Nagpur there is no shortage of available land, but a shortage of cleared land or of labour to clear new land (Yorke 1976: 41).

[2]McDougal refers to Christoph von Fürer-Haimendorf (1950) who suggests in his comparative survey that this institution seems to be unique to the Juang and the culturally similar Hill Bhuiya, whereas single-sex (male) youth dormitories are said to be more common in tribal peninsular and Himalayan India (ibid.). Cf. also Gell on the *Muria Gond of Bastar* in this chapter, who have a mixed-sex dormitory or *ghotul* (Gell 1992: 149).

classification, structure, and social interaction, he analyses the inner make-up of Juang family and kinship patterns, of the marriage and age systems, and of economic, ritual and political organization of territory and clan.[3] McDougal's bibliography lists titles from 1961, but, perhaps following his theoretical approach, not the studies of van Gennep and Hertz, both of which had been translated into English by then.

The discussion in the previous chapter has been about notions of death and dying and how a given society and its social order are regenerated in the structured components of the funerary rituals. McDougal's analysis, however, focuses on the structural core and present state of Juang society rather than on its ideological renewal, for example, in death rituals. His concern is with the living, and, due to his structural-functional approach, with how the functioning of their secular and ritual institutions contributes to the societal whole. Matters related to the social afterlife of the Juang remain vague. It might also be argued that he does not conceive of death as being an integral part of life and consequently does not look for any kind of social order or structure in it.[4] Family ceremonies, village and a number of other ceremonies including the description of one funeral are presented as structurally similar procedures in the analysis of which minor importance is attached to ethnographic detail.[5]

Still, there are a few hints indicating that the world of the dead is of ritual importance in Juang society.

ANCESTORS

The recent dead are referred to 'as ghosts and also ancestors, . . . a class of supernaturals' (McDougal 1963: 331). It remains unclear, however, how a potentially dangerous ghost is cere-

[3]These are some of the headings taken from the table of contents of McDougal's monograph.

[4]Sahlins, in contrast, analyses the social order, hierarchy or organization of the spirit world as being modelled on the social structure of the living (Sahlins 1968: 18). Cf. also Vitebsky who dedicates a complete chapter to the 'social order among the dead' (Vitebsky 1993: 132).

[5]Cf. the discussion of the funeral ceremony in this chapter.

monially taken care of and eventually transformed into an ancestor. The period of transition takes about twenty years (ibid.);[6] after that a deceased is no longer considered a ghost. It is assumed, however, that a person continues to 'exercise influence on the living' (ibid.) after death. Individual and collective ancestors are regularly given offerings and included in rituals. In Hill Juang ancestry female ancestors are included. All ancestors are addressed in family or village rituals 'as long as they are remembered' (ibid.). However, female ancestors will not be named, and for that reason they are earlier forgotten.[7] All ancestors need to be regularly placated, because they may cause damage to crops, livestock, and the living, if displeased. Although ancestors are generally assumed to be benevolent to people, this seems to be a rather uncertain and relative concept.[8]

The vision of a cyclical renewal of Juang society or former generations comes alive in the name-giving ritual, in which a child is usually given the name of a deceased person in the generation of the child's father's father (ibid.: 99).

DEATH

In spite of not dealing explicitly with the ideology of death, McDougal almost in passing points out examples which reveal that death in Juang society is more than a 'technical' moment at the end of an individual's life. Ideas of (female) fertility, (male)

[6]This is a long journey, a period of almost one generation. For this reason I find it hard to imagine this transition as an unstructured, ritually almost empty and otherwise almost meaningless passage. At least the reader is not informed by McDougal about the stages of a ghost transforming into an ancestor, the relations between the living and the dead and the rituals of exchange between them. A second burial or its equivalent is not mentioned. All these might be aspects of some structural interest.

[7]Interestingly, this is an almost word-by-word rendering of what Deeney (3/unpubl.) has to say on the ancestor veneration of the Ho.

[8]This statement rings also fairly similar to the situation of the Sora. It seems that what McDougal calls 'ghosts' or 'malevolent ancestors' may be equivalent to the 'Experience *sonums*' in the case of the Sora (Vitebsky 1993).

sexuality, and the regeneration of society seem to be implied in Juang notions of death.[9]

(1) If in the case of the annual ceremonial hunt, for example, the hunting party is not successful, a ritual is performed. A successful hunt is considered necessary for the initiation of the new seasonal round of productive activities. So the married women of the village assemble. They are handed over the bows and arrows that will be redistributed to their owners eventually. Before leaving, one of the women pretends to die by falling down. She is 'reanimated' by one of the hunters. Only then may the hunting party set off a second time. On their successful return the men are ceremoniously blessed by the women. It may be argued then that female properties of fertility have brought about success in the hunt symbolizing the reproduction of life (cf. ibid.: 210 f.).

(2) The funeral ceremony[10] is an affair of two days beginning with the immediate cremation of the body on the first

[9]In terms of male and female polarity female fertility is opposed and complemented by male virility. The life-giving powers of human reproduction as well as plants and animals are attributed to women and dependent on the properties of female fecundity. There is no indication here of Bloch's differentiation between superior controlled male fertility and inferior uncontrolled female sexuality. On the contrary, McDougal discusses male sexuality as potentially harmful to reproductive processes.

[10]A rough grid of the funeral ceremony is described in three and a half pages concentrating on observable behaviour and ritual steps in chronological order. Ethnographic description of certain structurally interesting detail is lacking to the extent that one wonders whether McDougal has been an eye-witness to the scene. For example: in the context of the funeral 'the deceased's closest agnatic relative fashions a crude mud image representing the dead person' (McDougal 1963: 333). The Ho among whom I did fieldwork, have a similar custom. But with them, for example, half of the mud needed to create an effigy is taken from the southern part of the grave, the direction in which the head of the deceased is positioned (cf. Prologue), and the other half is brought from *outside* the soil of the deceased's homestead by male members of the local lineage, but from land *inside* the village boundaries. For the effigy the two

> day and finishing with a village feast sponsored by the family of the deceased on the second day. In the course of a rite materials are used which are ascribed certain purifying qualities such as water, chicken blood, oil, and egg yolk. The egg yolk may, perhaps, serve as a symbol of fertility hinting at renewal and growth at the moment of death. Oil in this ritual may function as a symbol of (an implied) marriage (ceremony), as death in tribal societies is often seen as an alliance and talked about in the language of marriage initiating a transition into a new phase[11] (cf. Otten 2006: 274).

Looking at who is involved in the funeral ceremony it becomes obvious that death is clearly recognized as a social event. One male from each family of the whole village is expected to assist for the full two days. The final purification ritual on the second day includes everybody involved in the funeral and affected by death pollution as well as the ghosts. Different categories of Juang society including their dead are united in these symbolic actions. They are performed by any male of the deceased's mother's brother's village. For this task someone from the category of the unmarried young boys is chosen. This category commands a positive ritual status similar to that of the ritual elders who in turn will be given an extra share in the final feast in which all of the villagers are included.

By associating the categories of unmarried young boys and ritual elders in the funeral ceremony, the cyclical view of Juang society is stressed. Also, the superior cultural, non-physical aspect of sexuality or fertility is underlined in the ritual since both categories are identified by their distance from or absence of their procreative biological capacities. There seems to be an

halves are worked into each other, forming one round ball from which eventually in the case of a dead male a man on horseback is modelled, in the case of a deceased female a mud-woman with a pile of firewood on her head is formed. The task of modelling the mud, in the case of the Ho, must not be done by anyone belonging to the same title as the deceased.

[11]Demmer points to both oil and turmeric being smeared on the pot with the deceased's soul in it (phase 3 of the Koya death ritual).

idea of death as a drawn out process (cf. Bloch 1988) when considering the extended transition period of turning into a Juang ancestor.

As could be shown there are important ties between the living and the dead in Juang society. However, little emphasis has been attached by McDougal to structural detail concerning the world of the dead and to the mourners coming to grips with the phenomenon of death – emotionally, socially, culturally. This is the focus of Vitebsky's monograph on the Sora, a tribe belonging to the same language family as the Juang, to which we now turn.

THE CONTINUATION OF CONSCIOUSNESS AFTER DEATH: THE SORA OF EASTERN MIDDLE INDIA

This discussion of Sora awareness of mortality is based on Piers Vitebsky's monograph (1993): *Dialogues with the Dead. The discussion of mortality among the Sora of eastern India.* According to his interpretation Sora ideology and praxis of death, loss, and the continuity of life and society is reflected and structured in multi-dimensional ways. Actually, the monograph is a sensitive elaboration of most of the aspects implied in the subject matter of this study in culturally sophisticated and, as Vitebsky claims, distinctively Sora ways.[12] Sora values and ideas operating within the framework of a holistic tribal society and the 'order of things' permeating the spheres of life, death, and the whole cosmos are illustrated in 'Dialogues with the Dead'. It

[12]Of course, it will be impossible to be sure if the Sora way of being nested in matters of *otherworldliness* is a 'distinctive Sora way' indeed and possibly (fundamentally) different in other tribal societies. Perhaps Vitebsky's perspective and focus on Sora spiritual, psychological and sociological life is responsible for what he was able to perceive and which ultimately became part of himself. One wonders what would/could be revealed about other ethnic categories if a similar approach was employed in the description and analysis of their cultures. What image and understanding would develop in the reader's mind if Vitebsky had done fieldwork among the Hill Juang, for example? How would the Sora have been portrayed differently if McDougal had been the ethnographer?

seems that Sora society is one 'where all things touch', but, of course, this is also a result of Vitebsky's subtle portrayal.

This chapter tries to reflect Vitebsky's fieldwork. For this it will focus on the 'two-way traffic which the Sora say passes constantly between the realms of life and death' (Vitebsky 1993: 236).

Vitebsky carried out long-term fieldwork among shamans and shifting cultivators in Middle India between 1976 and 1979.[13] He spent eighteen months in three different villages among the Sora of central India, learned their language and finally performed not as a shaman,[14] as he had originally intended and was invited to do, but as an *Ancestor-Man.*[15] He completed his PhD thesis about the Sora experience in 1982 and has published regularly on aspects of Sora political life, their ecology, cosmology and language between 1978 and 1993. Before his dissertation went to press the manuscript was dicussed in detail at a meeting of the Anthropology-Psychoanalysis Interdisciplinary Colloquium of the American Psychoanalytic Association in New York. In the last chapter Vitebsky draws a comparison between Sora ways of mourning and contemporary psychotherapy and psychoanalysis.

The Sora, in administrative terms an ST, are largely shifting cultivators,[16] but they also make a living by hunting, gathering,

[13]Vitebsky has been head of Anthropology and Russian Northern Studies at the Scott Polar Research Institute in Cambridge Great Britain since 1986. Since 1988 he has conducted fieldwork among nomadic reindeer herders in the Siberian Arctic. This and more information on the author is given on the website of the *Scott Polar Research Institute*, University of Cambridge.

[14]The main reason being his inability to receive the necessary teaching in his dreams and to perform the incestuous marriage with a high-caste cross-cousin of his patrilineage. These two prerequisites are essential in the making of a shaman (cf. Vitebsky 1993: 23).

[15]Much of the book's material is based on Vitebsky's participation in the role of the ancestor-man, for example during the seasonal harvest rites or in the course of funerals. 'Like any Sora, my experiences were made possible, and my own biography developed, by talking to the dead as well as to the living' (Vitebsky 1993: 23).

[16]For the complex of shifting cultivation cf. Chapter Four.

and 'settled' cultivation. They live in the hills of southern Orissa and Andhra Pradesh. Vitebsky stayed with the Lanjia Sora, the most isolated group of Sora settling along the mountainous border between Ganjam and Koraput district (cf. Appendix 4). There they live together with *Pano* (*Dom*) who trade with them and lend them money which the Sora need for the buffalo sacrifices, for example, functioning perhaps as the Soras' clients. The relations between Sora and *Pano* are characterized by both 'mutual distance and dependence' (Vitebsky 1993: 32).[17]

Relationships in the villages are close, and people have usually grown up together and known each other all of their lives. They will participate in each other's funerals. Men often stay in their villages for good, whereas women may come (those women who have married in from far away) and go (sisters who will marry outside). Interaction is not free of tension. In fact, tensions may be most extreme where closeness is most intense, for example among (lineage) brothers where 'sorcery is most likely' (ibid.: 38). In the social organization of the Sora, the absence of phratries and (totemic) clans is conspicuous, making them an exception in tribal Middle India.[18] In every village there are one or more exogamous local descent groups (*birinda*) containing a few households or nuclear families and operating according to patrilineal rules. Exogamy is counted in an egocentric manner,[19] and as long as women marry outside their lineage, marriages are possible inside and outside the village. Ego's parallel cousins are addressed as 'brothers' and 'sisters' and as such they are not marriageable. Moreover, ego is supposed to address his cross-cousins as 'brothers' and 'sisters' as well, and for three generations intermarriage should be avoided. In practice this may happen, though, but the situation is highly sensitive and such marriages

[17]Cf. Chapter Two for the discussion of status, ritual purity, and the relation between patrons and clients in tribal societies.

[18]'Totemic' is enclosed in brackets, since the Ho, for instance, recognize a clan level of social structure, but only to a very limited degree one of the totemic kind.

[19]This is pointed out by Pfeffer (2002b: 68). Also, there are 'extensive affinal regulations offer[ing] terms of order and orientation beyond the individual neighbourhood.' (Pfeffer 2002a: 8)

are not always accepted. There is a notion of ambiguity about cross-cousins in general and one of incest in particular about their inter-marrying, since 'brother' and 'sister' are felt to be terms reserved for one's own lineage. But according to Vitebsky there is a 'culturally powerful fantasy about marriage between brother and sister' (ibid.: 60). It plays an important role in Sora myth, and also the concept of Sora shamanism is born from and within the framework of 'brother'–'sister' incest. At this superior ritual level, superior status is attached by relations of incest. Similarly, in terms of ritual purity a female shaman *must* always be married to a 'cross-cousin' and 'brother'[20] of high *kshatriya varna* in the Underworld.

Vitebsky states that before he went to Sora country he had never seen a corpse, and to him contemplating death and dying had been an interior and mental process taking place in his mind, if at all. Seen from the perspective of a Sora individual, however, death and the dead are issues of public interaction and negotiation. They are exterior issues that cannot be evaded in everyday life. Moreover, in practice there is a subtle system of classification as it concerns the different categories of the dead[21] who are supposed to dwell in known sites of the joint landscape. So, when living persons are walking around inside and outside their villages they may encounter *sonums,*[22] since it is publicly known that and where they reside in springs, forests, rocks, and other conspicuous features of the surroundings. This encounter may well be dangerous. In terms of the landscape Vitebsky speaks of a 'gigantic three-dimensional mnemonic device' (Vitebsky 1993: 75). The visible environment is complemented by an equally real and invisible one, which the Soras pass without fear, but with a 'keen awareness of mutual dependence' (ibid.: 81). Another example may illustrate the interweaving between the living and the dead: whenever Sora people are eating (grain) they are seen to be in their ancestors' company because it is

[20]As in the case of shamanism, Sora like to talk about their dead in terms of kinship. Vitebsky criticizes Elwin (1955) sharply for failing to see the sociological grounding of Sora ideology, for example, in their social organization.

[21]Cf. paragraph 'Sonum: the construction of the dead' in this chapter.

[22]When a person dies, s/he will eventually become (a) *sonum*.

assumed that ancestors have contributed their soul-force to the grain.[23] This is considered a benign and obliging act, again stressing the idea of mutual dependence. Ancestors in their 'nourishing' aspect are symbolically linked in Sora awareness with the (re-)sources of all that is passed down via inheritance. When, as a third example, a Sora person falls ill, again the dead are involved, as it is believed that illness is caused by them;[24] with the help of a healing shaman the dead become audible and display their matter-of-fact character. In the course of funeral rituals and seasonal ceremonies so-called ancestor-men and ancestor-women not only perform as ancestors, they actually become these ancestors and subsequently have to be ritually dissociated. So the invisible world of the dead is very real: it is active, concrete, and in an exterior way permanently present in people's lives.

BASIC SORA IDEAS OF LIFE AND DEATH

Vitebsky's monograph is about Sora spirituality and the sophisticated entwinement of roughly half a million living Sora with their dead. The issue of death figures prominently in their lives, and to them death is not a negation or absence of life or an end to being active: the kind of communication will certainly have

[23]With the Sora there is also a system of classification as concerns the fate of a 'soul' or 'consciousness'. There is a 'soul' called *puradan* animating humans and also animals and plants. Distinct from this is the 'soul' called *kulman* relating to the period between a person's death and the stone-planting ceremony (*guar*). Vitebsky translates *kulman* also as 'ghost'. The different stages of a dead person after the stone-planting ceremony are assigned different kinds of 'souls' called *sonums*. The soul-force re-infused into the grain by an *ancestor sonum* is called *puradan* implying that the dead have returned to the living and that their relation is one of reciprocal nourishment. This notion is 'rooted in a basic image of kinship' (ibid.: 54).

In the course of my fieldwork among the Ho my Santal assistant pointed out that although children in tribal society generally grow up fairly free, parents will insist from a very early age that they do not spill rice grains on the floor when eating, in order not to annoy their ancestors.

[24]For the dangerous aspect of ancestors in the form of Experience *sonums* see later in this chapter.

to change, but interaction will continue and the Sora have concrete ways and means of solving that difficulty. In long-running discussions of up to several hours over disputes and animosities, uncertainties about the relationships between the living and the dead are gradually and painfully settled. There is no concept of a 'natural' death, so when someone dies, or falls ill for that matter, there will be a number of enquiries into the cause of that death or that particular disease. A Sora person is an accumulation of relationships with other Sora persons including the dead, and Vitebsky speaks of a 'complex web of interrelational or mutual agency' (Vitebsky 1993: 9) that every Sora person finds himself in and that bears upon a person's viability as well as his vulnerability. Death and illness are believed to be caused by an irritation or flaw in these relations, the awareness of the dead (or the lack of it) being an integral part of the physical state of a Sora person. Sora do not believe in death causing a particular person's annihilation, but a separation affecting (not finishing off) the relationship with the living. There are varying degrees and modes of being dead in which the dead are supposed to be verbally articulate. Death, like life, is seen as only a phase in the total existence of a Sora person. The relations between the Sora and their dead remain close and active. They are dialectic insofar as the dead are transformed in the course of the 'dialogues' by the living, just as the living are subject to a process of a non-linear evolution as brought about by the deceased. In the course of their lives *and* their deaths, the Sora undergo structured transitions positioning them in cosmologically well-defined communal time and space. Psychological and sociological dimensions are interwoven in the Sora process of mourning their dead (and themselves). It is a process which is internal as well as external, always public and verbal, since the dialogues between the living and the dead are mediated and verbalized by (often female) shamans in trance. These continuing conversations take place in every Sora village, sometimes several times a day. The communicative process is clearly not a one-way road. It may be one of struggle and negotiation, the quality and intensity of which is actively determined by both sides in unpredictable ways. For the deceased it may be a long journey of more than two generations before distressing uncertainties have been settled, before they will cease being dangerous and gradually become benevolent ancestors, eventually turn speechless, pass on their names, die a second death in the underworld, turn into a butterfly (an a-verbal being that can neither be addressed nor speak actively itself), and may finally be forgotten.

It will have become clear by now how intensely death related matters are woven into Sora secular and ritual life. Even for analytical reasons it seems almost impossible to draw a dividing line between life and death as two separate realms.

A closer look at the formation of the Sora person, at the construction of the dead as *sonums* and the process of *making* ancestors will follow. Related to this are particular funerary rites; the second burial (*guar*) will be discussed, as Vitebsky calls this ceremony the key to the funeral.[25] I am aware, however, that by choosing some aspects and neglecting others I am artificially dissecting things that conceptually belong together.

THE SORA CONCEPT OF THE PERSON

Resuming the discussion of the notion of the *dividuum* by M. Bloch[26] the focus is now on the Sora concept of the person.

[25] I concentrate on these major aspects as I do not want to repeat what Kottmann (1999) did when giving a fairly detailed description of Sora culture primarily based on Vitebsky's work, but also taking Elwin's book on the Sora into account (Elwin 1955). This had inspired Vitebsky to do fieldwork among the Sora in the first place. The sophisticated interrelatedness and tangled intertwining of Sora ideas and values, of 'lineage, property, inheritance, love, jealousy and anger, . . . of a person's cosmological position and his state of mind' (Vitebsky 1993: 12) may be assumed from the fact that Kottmann needs to 'hop around' collecting bits and pieces that are dispersed all over the place within Vitebsky's monograph in his effort to establish a different kind of systematic order and logic and come up with a more 'readable' version. Vitebsky obviously wanted to deal with things within the lived socio-cultural context as defined from the Sora point of view. So he abstained from chapter headings such as *Economy, Ecology, Religion, Social Organization, Life-cycle,* or *Funeral Rites*. If this is the kind of approach that readers prefer because this pigeon-holing better fits their own logic they may be at a loss and may want to resort to Vitebsky's detailed index instead or to Kottmann or both.

[26] Bloch had pointed out the necessity of discussing the concept of the person in a given culture 'before explaining what happens at death' (Bloch 1988: 15).

Everything in Sora society seems to be related to or based on it. 'The concept of *sonum* amounts to a total social fact' (Vitebsky 1993: 13), and in this paragraph the concept of *sonum* is integrated into the Sora concept of the person.

> The person appears more as a confluence which comes together only on the basis of its relationship to other beings who are themselves equally changing. Just as persons and other entities radiate something of themselves out to others, so they seem to be hard to bring and hold together: their constituent elements tend to drift away again and go towards the formation of other entities. (Vitebsky 1993: 46)

In this light a person is interpreted as an entity having at his centre a core, and diffusing at its outer edges into other persons, living *and* dead. This is a statement of enormous practical consequences bearing on people's behaviour in their everyday lives. Virtually everything happening to or concerning someone may be seen as caused by one's cumulative involvement with other persons whose actions will be interpreted as 'contagious' and potentially dangerous. Already at a very early stage the formation of a foetus in the womb is susceptible to other *sonums* and persons beyond his/her parents. This is why a Sora woman will avoid certain people, places, and food during her pregnancy.

A Sora person is believed to pass through several stages in the course of her/his existence, i.e. before, during, and after life. The stages of a dead person and the gradual process of dying concern the period of time extending from a person's first death on earth to the second death in the Underworld. Interpreting the second death as the final dissolution of a Sora person, the complete life-cycle of a Sora comprises three consecutive generations. The necessary changes involved in the evolution of the dead are never accomplished in one step. They may be time-consuming, painful and full of conflicts. They 'struggle' into effect 'only gradually and against the persistence of the previous state' (ibid.: 46). In other words: a change in status or into a newly acquired stage may always also be reversed and the person may be thrown back into a former stage. A reversal, for instance, takes place in the case of a stillbirth or in the case of a *sonum* changing back and forth between a benevolent ancestor and an aggressive Experience *sonum*.

SONUM: THE CONSTRUCTION OF THE DEAD

Vitebsky claims that 'the word *sonum* represents the most enigmatic stage of personhood' (ibid.: 9). His book may be seen as an elaboration of the elaborate Sora classification of this 'total social fact'. The category of *sonum* is charged with associations, meanings, content and connotations. A *sonum* is an entity, a state, a (relational) concept, a transitional category, a principle of causality in human affairs, and the main agent.

To gain a preliminary and rough idea of the Sora concept of a *sonum*, some significant characteristics will be listed. This does not suggest any sort of linear sequence, however. It may help us understand why Vitebsky decided to come up with a translation of *sonum* as Memory only *after* a subtle analysis of the relations between the living and the dead.[27]

1. Nothing in a person's fate is interpreted as solely innate, and this holds also true for a dead person. So a person's death does not just happen (due to biological factors or old age: these would be 'solely innate' reasons), it must have been caused[28] by his or her involvement with other *sonums*.
2. *Sonum* is a generic term. Depending on a *sonum's* particular stage within the life-cycle and the relationship between a *sonum* and the living, the term is specified in manifold ways.
3. The fate of a *sonum* is linked to the biography of living persons and their feelings about them.
4. The *sonum* of someone recently deceased is assumed to

[27]Vitebsky criticizes Elwin for having interpreted *sonum* as god, spirit, and deity. Elwin's gloomy portrayal of Sora society in which the living are permanently oppressed by the dead/gods/spirits/deities would have been sparked off by his translation and understanding of what a *sonum* is. For half of the book Vitebsky's preliminay translation of *sonum* is 'the continuation of consciousness after death'.

[28]According to Vitebsky, in Sora society the principle of causality is recognized. It is of paramount importance and serves as a guideline when it comes to exploring a *kulman's* or *sonum's* motivation and state of mind in the course of the dialogues. Why did somebody die (and how)? Why is (a) *kulman/sonum* aggressive? Why do they want to 'eat' the living?

exist in a state of sensual and material deprivation and needs to be 'fed' by both sacrifice and communication. In this mode a *sonum* is suffering and deserves and demands compassion.

5. *Sonums* 'behave' in contradictory ways. On the one hand they are believed to inflict upon others the experiences that led to their own painful deaths. The image in this context is that of 'eating' or absorbing the soul of the living:[29] they attack the living, they are dangerous, harmful, and aggressive. They are causal agents. This category of *sonum* is called Experience *sonum*, comprising a collectivity of people who have died similar deaths and have experienced similar pain.
6. On the other hand, *sonums* are protective and nurturing too. As the land is given to the living by their ancestors, the living feel obliged to the dead.[30] This relation between *sonums* and the living is acknowledged as a nourishing one. This category of *sonum* is called Ancestor *sonum*.
7. The living and the dead in their Experience mode are linked by their shared victimhood in an analogy of suffering. Successful ancestorhood is free of this self-centredness.
8. *Sonums* are verbally articulate. They speak directly through the mouth of a shaman to the living. The shaman does not add to or comment on what is being said. She is nothing but a channel, a technical means enabling the process of dialogue.
9. *Sonums* tell the living the cause of their death, their state of mind, and what they are up to. Their claims on the living are acknowledged by these as a matter of principle.
10. An Experience *sonum* needs to be redeemed before s/he can pass through the transitional category of Earth *sonum* and eventually turn into an Ancestor *sonum*.

[29]The change in attitude is also reflected in the language. As the living will refer to the situation by making use of transitive verbs in the passive voice ('I will be grabbed, I will be eaten'), Experience *sonums* are referred to in the active voice ('I will eat you, I will grab you').

[30]As mentioned above, ancestors sustain the living also by enlivening their grain with their soul-force.

11. The nature of Earth *sonums* is dualistic. Earth *sonums* are Experience *sonums* and as such dangerous. Earth *sonums* are also half way in a person's transition to Ancestor *sonum*. They are assumed to reside in springs; in fact there are as many Earth sites 'across the landscape as there are springs and water holes' (Vitebsky 1993: 220).
12. To each category of *sonum* is attributed a distinctive cosmological position and environmental feature in the landscape, known to the living. This positioning is, however, provisional, temporary, and reversible, depending on the state of the relationships between the living and the dead.
13. The (necessary) redemption of the dead will be enhanced by so-called ancestor-men and ancestor-women dancing and singing for the dead in the course of the funeral as much as by the medium of dialogue. The funeral is a crucial step in a person's transformation.
14. The transformative biography of a *sonum* is cosmological, as s/he will be moved around the landscape: there are different sites available for conflicting Earth *sonums*; an Ancestor's *sonum* may be thrown back into the stage of an Experience *sonum*. Accordingly, their locations in the landscape will change. The transformative process is also seen as ontological, since they will be turned from one kind of *sonum* into another, and most importantly as social, since they will leave the anti-society of the Experience victims and join the company of their patrilineal ancestors (ibid.: 11). Ancestors are associated with values such as social responsibility, collectivity, lineage, solidarity, and sustenance.
15. The ambiguous status of women is reflected in the choice of the Earth site that they must make. Although married women are given a second stone-planting at their natal village,[31] it is a matter of negotiation and some consequence whether they will settle after death in the Earth

[31]Men are given one stone-planting, just as unmarried women, by the lineage into which they were born.

site of their husbands or in that of their paternal Ancestor *sonums*.

16. An Ancestor *sonum* whose redemption is complete will no more revert to the stage of the Experience *sonum*. In this mode their names will be passed on to a new-born baby. The name-giving procedure thus reflects an important step in the process of a *sonum's* transformation, free of aggression. It is a symbol or a hard-won social identity constitutive of the purely constructive role of Ancestor *sonum*.

According to Vitebsky's analysis the dialogues reflect the mood of the dead as well as that of the living. Although *sonums* seem to have autonomy this is a relative one since it depends on the living and their memories of the dead. These memories are interspersed with projections of their own thoughts and feelings into the dead. In the course of the dialogues unresolved affairs and relationships are sorted out, negotiated, and disputed. It is because of the public and collective nature of the dialogues that the Sora 'therapy' of settling feelings and moods becomes externalized and 'objective'. This process is fundamentally different from the Western concept of psychoanalysis and psychotherapy, Vitebsky argues, according to which the process of coming to grips with someone's death may be also a verbal one, but is seen primarily as private, individual, subjective.[32]

As the memory of every dead Sora person is debated in a public arena, it reflects an autonomous reality outside the mind of the rememberer(s). To visualize the difference from a Western memory set within the internal mind of the rememberer, Vitebsky translates *sonum* as Memory.

FUNERAL CYCLE AND *GUAR* (THE PLANTING OF THE STONE)

As Vitebsky treats the Sora notion of *sonum* as a 'total social fact', all the chapters in his book are related to this concept or aspects of it in one way or another. A *sonum* does not come into existence at a person's physical death but is very much alive and

[32]Cf. Prologue and Chapter One.

real throughout the life-span. Perhaps this is the reason why Vitebsky chose not to come up with a separate chapter on the sequence of Sora funerary rites. He explains, however, that they are important for the continuity of Sora society and contribute to reconstituting in the Underworld a social order modelled on that existing among the living.[33]

The formal stages of the funeral process take three years, beginning with the cremation of the body immediately after death and continuing with three collective annual harvest commemorations or *karja* ontologically advancing the dead as Experience *sonums* in the course of the funeral cycle into an Ancestor *sonum*. Even after three years this evolution of a dead does not always seem to be completed. Vitebsky argues that it will only be accomplished when the deceased's name has been passed on to a successor (in a ceremony full of joy and laughter, ibid.: 226), and this may take anything between three and a hundred years. In this light the name-giving ceremony is the final and crucial stage of the funeral cycle.

Ancestors will eventually be able to die their second death in the Underworld (after having passed on land, grain, crops, and their name to the living), when their rememberers die their first deaths. This implies basically that 'one remains affected by all one's Memories for the rest of one's life' (ibid.: 237).

The 'stone-planting ceremony' (*guar*) takes place weeks or months after a person's first burial. It is a complex ritual in the course of which a rock is set, chants are sung, buffaloes are sacrificed and the second inquest of the deceased is carried through. All of this is performed within one day, involving a deceased person's lineage members and affines in prescribed and separate ways. It is the central rite within the funeral cycle (ibid.: 11, 49, 70, 121 and 225). For the deceased the second burial indicates an irreversible transformation towards a *sonum*,

[33]Although there seems to be no doubt about the cyclic view of Sora society the analogy between the world of the living and the Underworld of the ancestors is not free of contradictions. It is rather a 'topsy-turvy parody' (ibid.: 217) with seasons, days and nights reversed. On the other hand, there is a social life after death: marriage, drinking and sleeping with others, buffaloes helping with the harvest, etc.

as they will stop being inarticulate and confused ghosts (*kulman*). The qualities of this stage are clearly assessed as negative, also because *sonums* need to be verbally fit and must have a clear mind. This is because their final and future transition into a pure ancestor depends on solving pending uncertainties in the course of further dialogues. On that day ancestor-men not only act, but actually become Ancestors.[34] They represent the lineage of the dead and underline its continuity by enumerating all ancestors of all the lineage's branches by name. The focus of the whole procedure is clearly on the lineage rather than on the individual dead, although the ancestor-to-be is invited to join their company of ancestor *sonum*. It is because of the words chanted by the ancestor-men on the occasion of the stone-planting that they contribute to the deceased's redemption. The transformation into an ancestor, however, is still provisional, intended and wished for rather than accomplished on that day. This will leave the relations between the living and the dead even after the second burial unsettled and under strain. The two-way traffic continues.

Ancestor *sonums* are allocated ancestor space, which is associated in Sora awareness with the Underworld, the house of the deceased, and the space within the village. An ancestor will continue to have access to the world of the living: to the house and the grain kept in the storage room of the respective lineage category via the mortar set in the floor, to the village and his respective earth sites via the rocks or stones set for him at his *guar*.

On behalf of the dead, buffaloes are sacrificed, which serve as a substitute for the donors, saving them from the attacks of the dead in their mode as Experience *sonum*. There are three different categories of buffalo-givers depending on their closeness to or distance from the deceased, and Vitebsky points out the difference in behaviour of the members of a lineage and that of the affines (ibid.: 184). The immediate heirs of a dead person are entitled to their inheritance only after planting the stone, providing a buffalo, 'sacrificing' an egg or eating a 'cremated' rice-flour effigy of the dead, thus claiming the name of the deceased for one of their descendants (ibid.: 71). The ancestor will have

[34]Cf. no. 13 on 'ancestor-men' earlier in this chapter.

acquired full rights of residence in the house/s of this lineage category of heirs. Other lineage members may also 'hit a buffalo' (*id-bong*), but will not give an egg or eat the effigy signifying they have no rights towards the deceased's property, land, or name. Affines,[35] on the other hand, will 'dance a buffalo' (*tongseng-bong*): they will perform a kind of 'war' dance[36] as the 'affinal act *par excellence*' (ibid.: 72). Analogous to the classification of *sonums* there exists a classification of those attending a funeral determining their specific behaviour, their rights and duties, and their future relationship with the dead.

In Sora society, then, the circumstances of each person are thoroughly explored in life and after dying. However, there is hardly anything individual about this process, and Vitebsky argues that 'the ultimate nature of a dead person's transformation is a social one' (ibid.: 132). Likewise, the rituals accompanying this transformation work towards a continuity of the kin-based social order of the respective lineage and Sora society as a whole.[37] The dead in the social and protective mode of ancestor

[35]Again, participating cross-cousins are expected to 'dance the buffalo' that way enacting their role as affines or outsiders to the lineage.

[36]Among the Ho I witnessed the arrival of the 'affines' in the course of the preparations for a wedding, in that case the arrival of the bridegroom, his *mamu* and their party. They tried to 'invade' the territory of the bride in an almost violent way which reminded me of the war-dance that Vitebsky describes here in the case of a second burial. Contrary to 'mainstream' Ho custom, the wedding in this case took place at the bridal site (*diku andi*), and only after the completion of the wedding rituals did the couple set off to the groom's place.

[37]In the course of the stone planting ceremony in some villages an effigy of the deceased is made from a handful of grains that each participating household contributes (thus underlining the social character of the ceremony). Later this effigy is 'cannibalized' according to a set of fixed rules determining who may eat it and who may not (thus reflecting the social structure among lineage members and affines). Excluded from eating are unmarried women past puberty (who belong to the lineage of the deceased and are supposed to later marry outside), since in their case this would be interpreted as an act of paternal incest and they would be believed to turn sterile. Children and all males of the lineage are allowed to consume the effigy (thus acting out their roles in the public performance of a social drama dealing with the topics of sexuality, fecundity, and progeny).

sonum play a crucial role in this by enacting the cyclic regeneration of Sora society and linking the living and the dead in symbolic ways:

- by ingesting the deceased person's soul in the shape of the sacrificed buffalo, for example, who is then supposed to live on in the living;
- by ingesting the ancestor('s soul) in the shape of grains;
- in the naming ceremony the ancestor becomes a component of the baby's person;
- ancestors are allocated fixed residential sites among the living.

Ancestors represent Sora society's 'partial triumph over death' (ibid.: 226) by leaving behind aspects of biology and individuality[38] and by their becoming associated with the creation of social identity and with tribal values of solidarity, prosperity, permanence, and fertility.

What are the relations between the living and the dead in Sora society? The dichotomy between life and death is a fact, though not in terms of a temporal sequence. Both notions are intertwined to the extent that one cannot speak of a conceptualization of life and one of death. There is basically one concept encompassing both notions and the entire cosmos. In a Sora person's life there are numerous situations and transitions in which the living actually represent/turn into/become/are (aspects of) the dead or vice versa. In Hertz's study the souls of the dead are analysed as a dangerous factor, an analytical or structural element. As such they are 'good to think', yet remain pale and 'lifeless'. In Vitebsky's monograph the Sora persons, living and dead, are depicted in their complexity, their autonomy and their agency. 'Dialogues with the dead', he says, 'are not about death, but about life: it is only by having a vision of what it is to be dead that one can have an understanding of what it is to be alive' (ibid.: 259).

[38]This may be concluded from the fact that the transformation into an overall benevolent ancestor is possible only after the uncertainties about an individual's physical death have been settled and a verdict reached.

DEATH AND THE RECONSTRUCTION OF KOYA SOCIETY IN SOUTHERN ORISSA

In a brief paper Ulrich Demmer (2007: 185–201) discusses ritual performances of Koya kin and affines in a situation of death. The Koya, also called Bison Horn Maria, are a Gondide tribe of slash-and-burn cultivators and cattle herders settled in the Malkangiri district in southern Orissa[39] and also in the eastern parts of Bastar. Koya society is kinship based and so is their system of social organization. There are totemic exogamous phratries and patrilineal clans. Phratries intermarry, whereas marriage within phratries or clans is prohibited. Accordingly, ego is rooted in a classificatory system distinguishing between categories of marriageable affines or *akomama* and non-marriageable fraternal clans or *dadabhai*.

This needed to be said since Demmer argues that Koya death rituals have a social (and moral) dimension. Affinity is a key value in Koya society and a key social principle organizing Koya society as a whole and its social and ritual life. So what is actually performed in the course of Koya death rituals are kinship relations, especially affinal ties, and acts of social memory of the deceased. Drawing from much the same literature discussed in Chapters One and Three of this study,[40] Demmer characterizes death in Koya society as a volatile act endangering the identity of Koya society as a 'social body of security, solidarity, and exchange' (Demmer 2007: 192). Death rituals are a means of coming to terms with someone's death as well as re-establishing constructive relationships with the dead by reintegrating them into society.

The three different phases of death ritual among the Koya are the cremation rites immediately after death, the 'stone setting' ceremony or *kallu padum*, and the ritual of bringing back the dead person's soul or *hanal jiva*.

In his brief ethnographic description Demmer confines himself

[39]For Malkangiri, the site of Demmer's fieldwork, cf. Appendix 4. For the technical term of 'slash-and-burn cultivation' see Chapter Four.

[40]Dumont (1986), Hertz (1907), van Genepp (1909), Bloch and Parry (1982), and Pfeffer (1991).

to demonstrate the overall presence and impact of affinal actors in each of the three phases: announcing death, assembling other relatives, carrying, placing and cremating the body (phase 1); digging the hole for the stone, sitting on the stone and setting the stone; sacrificing the buffalo, beating the drums (phase 2); rubbing turmeric and oil on a pot with the deceased's soul in it, performing more sacrifices (phase 3). This is interesting indeed, as with the Koya steps within the ritual are performed by affines, for example all the activities of the first phase, which are enacted by members of the dead person's lineage in the case of the Sora and by members of the entire village in the case of the Juang. Also, on the occasion of setting the stone in Sora ritual, affines (from other villages) are symbolically kept at a distance from lineage members by having them camp and eat outside the village boundaries. They are excluded from participating in other performances too, such as ingesting the dead person's soul in the form of an effigy or cake, or by 'hitting the buffalo'.

By pointing out the degree of affinal involvement[41] Demmer conveys the impression that lineage members only play a minor role. But then, certainly, crucial elements could not have been considered at all within the limited scope of Demmer's essay, elements which may relate to the dead person's category of non-affinal kin or *dadabhai*: matters of inheritance and the enumeration of the ancestors, for instance. It is amazing, however, that the reader is not informed about the period of time that the performances of the complete funeral rituals consume, in particular about the interval between the first funeral and the second, since this is an important moment in Hertz's line of argument.

Thus among the Koya the role of the affines' involvement seems to be an entirely constructive one of 'solidarity and support' (Demmer 2007: 197), at least as Demmer portrays it, whereas in Vitebsky (1993) and McDougal (1963) et al. a potential air of ever-present hostility is implied when it comes to dealing with

[41]For an overall understanding it may be interesting to learn how affines and lineage members are affected by death pollution and cope with it in different ways, also how men and women deal with it in different ways.

akomama or affinal kin. Also, Demmer speaks of the deceased participating actively in the future lives of the living. Perhaps Koya dead do not reach that degree of activity and autonomy that Sora ancestors are ascribed by Vitebsky, but Demmer's references to the Koya dead with the impersonal pronoun 'it' rings suspicious, suggesting the absence of sex, gender, and agency. The notion of death and the concept of *dividuum* so far had conveyed the idea of death resulting in finalizing one (biological) aspect of a (social) person, whereas other essential elements of the person would continue. A person, according to this understanding, would be transformed at death, but would not cease to exist. Consequently, one might argue, a dead person should be grammatically treated as complete and alive and referred to by the personal pronouns such as 'he/him', 'she/her'.

ESCHATOLOGY AND THE MURIA GOND OF BASTAR

The following is not a comprehensive presentation of one more tribal community in Middle India, but a selective discussion of the very few aspects related to the topic of death and dying or the relationship between the living and the dead that Simeran M.S. Gell has contributed in her monograph on the Muria of Bastar, like the Koya a branch of the Gond.[42]

Over a period of 21 months Gell stayed in M.,[43] a village in northern Bastar in an area to the east of where the Hill Maria settle (Appendix 4). Gill did fieldwork at very much the same time when Vitebsky stayed with the Sora. Gell's book *The Ghotul in Muria Society* is the revised version of her doctoral thesis of 1984 about the mixed-sex youth dormitory[44] as a distinctive cultural institution of far-reaching social consequences and village politics.

[42]S. Gell, from Punjab, conducted her fieldwork in central India together with her husband, Alfred Gell, then a reader in anthropology at the London School of Economics. In 1992, at the time of the publication of the monograph, S. Gell was a Research Associate in the Department of Social Anthropology, University of Cambridge.

[43]I don't give the name because Gell makes use of a pseudonym.

[44]For cultural variations of dormitories, see the description of the Hill Juang earlier in this chapter.

In administrative terms the Muria are one of 53 sub-divisions of the category of the Gond constituting the largest tribal *ethnos*[45] of India. The Muria have complex relations with the tribe of the Hill Maria and the Maraar, the largest Hindu caste group. The Muria, according to Gell, situate themselves somewhere between these two. The Muria rank themselves higher than the Maria in terms of status. As is the case with many other tribal communities in India, Muria, Gond, and Maria are 'invented' designations used only by outsiders, whereas the Muria refer to themselves (and the Maria) as *koitor* meaning 'human beings' (Gell 1992: 2), distinguishing themselves from non-*koitor* categories such as the Maraar. Muria and Maraar live in the same villages in an atmosphere of mutual distrust; both keep socially and ritually segregated; also in terms of language, customs, and residence they are separate (ibid.: 78).[46] The Muria inhabit the plateau and the hilly regions of northern Bastar, an administrative district and the largest and most south-easterly within Madhya Pradesh, itself the largest state of India containing the largest population of tribal communities in the country. Bastar is a predominantly tribal area 'without considerable influx of Hindu peasants' (Skoda 2005: 174), and culturally diverse 'with many different groups living alongside each other' (Gell 1992: 13), both tribal and caste groups. Gell describes the Muria as a sedentary and, in their self-image, autochthonous tribe with permanent village

[45]Apart from the official administrative categorization beyond anthropological classification many different tribes conceive of themselves as Gond people, so the Greek term *ethnos* denoting 'a people' has been resorted to (cf. Pfeffer 2002a: 67).

[46]This absence of ritual interaction is a deviation from the Middle Indian pattern of the relation of interdependence between the tribal landowners and members of the Scheduled Castes cooperating ritually and economically as clients.

Also, among the Ho of Manbir members of the Scheduled Castes spoke Ho among each other and did not resort to it as a *lingua franca*; they mourned and buried their dead very much (though not completely) in Ho ways, mixed socially and ritually with the Ho. They had their houses built close to those of the Ho, though painted in different colours outside and were thus recognizable as Non-Ho. They lived scattered all over the village and not in a separate area.

sites and fields. Their diversified economy is one of shifting[47] and 'settled' cultivation, a mixture of gathering, hunting, rice-cultivation and the growing of other crops which carry ritual value (such as particular kinds of lentils or *pupulku,* ibid.: 32).

Just as Vitebsky was critical of Elwin's publication on the Sora for separating Sora shamanism and *sonums* from their social context, Gell criticizes Elwin's account of the Muria *ghotul* (Elwin 1947)[48] for similar reasons. Like Elwin, Gell identifies the 'ghotul as the key institution in Muria society' (Gell 1992: 20), but according to Gell because it reflects the pattern of Muria social life and Muria social organization (ibid.: 38). Basically, Gell's criticism aims at Elwin's not situating the *ghotul* in its sociological setting and speculating about it as a 'dreamland of adolescent sexual bliss' (ibid.: 21), ignoring its structural opposition and relatedness to the Muria system of alliance and affinity.

Similar to the Koya system of social organization, the Muria classify their social universe into kin or *dadabhai* categories and affinal or *saga* categories. However, despite the moiety arrangement of villages and the clear-cut dualism of *saga* and *dadabhai* categories at the highest level of the phratries, Gell points to the ambiguity and ambivalence of Muria social structure on the local(-ized clan segment) level, which she characterizes as 'maddeningly fluid and arbitrary' (ibid.: 38) and Pfeffer as apparently 'locally mixed up' and 'confusing' (Pfeffer 2002a: 67). Different exogamous clans are found residing in the villages. Due to Muria clans being both socio-centric and ego-centric categories at the same time, it may happen that a clan category that is classified by ego and his lineage in one village as falling in the *dadabhai* category may be considered *saga* in another village.[49] As the Muria social system is focused on marriage and as the clan system is considered a conceptual 'scheme for organizing

[47]For a brief elaboration of the term 'shifting cultivation' cf. Chapter Four.

[48]Pfeffer calls Elwin's monograph probably the 'best known ethnographic account of any Middle Indian tribe' (Pfeffer 1996: 101).

[49]Gell illustrates these conceptual complications by giving examples or case histories (Gell 1992: 60-2).

alliance' (Gell 1992: 61), Gell emphasizes a 'considerable social heterogeneity' (ibid.: 98). The *ghotul*-going boys and girls belong to the same age category, and because of the plurality of clan membership inside the villages it may well happen that inside a *ghotul* a girl will also come across boys falling into the category of predetermined affines or *saga*. It is for this reason that a girl is obliged to choose as her partner in the dormitory or *jor* a non-marriageable boy of her own moiety. As a result of her long-term fieldwork Gell is able to prove that the Muria institution of the *ghotul* is well set in 'the (Muria) order of things', i.e. in the Muria social system, and that deviations from the prescribed behaviour, e.g. pregnancies and elopements, will be clearly sanctioned.[50]

How are the relations between the living and the dead embedded in the Muria social system? And what vision is there in Muria society of a person's evolution after death? Gell's topic is a structural analysis of the socio-cultural institution of the *ghotul* as set within Muria social organization, based on and expressing distinctive tribal value-ideas of marriage and alliance. This is her focus, and in a subtle evaluation she successfully identifies Muria tribal society as a holistic society integrating spheres—ideologically isolated from each other or not existing at all in Western awareness—such as kin and affines, descent and alliance, gender-opposition (between husbands and wives, adolescent girls and boys), age-sets, generation and generational opposition, landscape and cultivation, status, and wealth and poverty into a meaningful whole.

Since no monograph will be comprehensive, the enlargement on crucial tribal issues such as matters of illness and healing,

---

Also, in this context Pfeffer points out the totemic classification of animal concepts which is reflected in the Gond system of distinguishing two levels of descent categories which are again 'similarly marked and coded by animal totems' (Pfeffer 2002a: 67).

[50]All of this—including Gell's characterization of *ghotul* relationships between boys and girls as generally 'mildly antagonistic' (Gell 1992: 211) rather than romantic or sentimental—fundamentally contradicts what Elwin had to say on the matter.

prominent rites and rituals (such as the seasonal, the life-cycle[51] and funeral rites), shamans and shamanism, creation myths and tribal gods, the transformation of the person at death, the process of turning into an ancestor and the interference by the dead in the lives of the living are not completely left out, but have been only briefly hinted at by Gell.

Still, it becomes clear that ancestors are allocated responsibility for the living. The role of an ancestor in the life of a Muria person coincides conceptually with what has been revealed about ancestors and the fate of the soul in the tribal societies discussed so far. There is a pantheon of village gods or *pen* presumed to reside in the forests outside the villages,[52] and it is to the *pen* and the forest that Muria ancestors are cosmologically linked. The forest is a spatial category and carries negative connotations as the realm of uncontrolled and uncontrollable nature, structurally the outside as seen from the perspective of the village. Also the feast to conclude the mortuary rite or *katar* is performed in the forest (ibid.: 29).

As in other tribal communities, in Muria eschatology ancestors are classified into malicious and benign ones. Contrary to how Demmer characterized the (harmonious) relations between kin and affines and similar to Vitebsky who described these as rather precarious among the Sora, Gell aligns malicious ancestors and *saga* or affines, who may communicate with each other (ibid.: 56–7) thereby posing a potential threat to a dead person's kin. For example, young Muria children grow up within the fenced boundaries of the nuclear or extended families, since children are '*susceptible* (my emphasis) to attack by ancestor

[51]Judging from the ethnographies I have studied so far I would have expected that in holistic tribal societies death and afterlife were considered stages within/of life and as such adequately ceremoniously dealt with. Gell, however, when referring to Muria life-cycle, lists the four stages as infancy and childhood (1), adolescence or the *ghotul* phase (2), married life or maturity (3), and old age (4), omitting death and the phase beyond.

[52]That is if they have left the Upper World and come down to earth in order to attend village festivals, for example, where they dance and enjoy themselves.

spirits who may be lurking around other people's houses' (ibid.: 125).[53]

Another distinction is made between the spirits of married and unmarried persons.[54] The spirits of men and married women usually dwell in the ancestral pots inside the partitioned area of a Muria house or storage place for grain and rice, which are considered to be controlled social and cultural sites. To this part of the house, daughters are forbidden entry during all of their lives (ibid.: 244). Within the spatial universe of the Muria, this controlled domestic site is opposed to the grazing land or *bhat*[55] where the spirits of unmarried women, 'whose links to lineage and clan via their husband remain unrealized are said to hover around' (ibid.: 36).[56] Muria ancestors will communicate with

[53]This is interesting for two reasons: (1) Vitebsky devoted a whole paragraph to the concept of 'destiny and susceptibility' (Vitebsky 1993: 63) when discussing the Sora formation of the person in order to show how already inside a mother's womb a Sora foetus is prone to a number of agents. (2) Among the Ho of Manbir I gained the impression that children from a very early age were allowed to roam around the village and the fields, bow and arrow usually at hand, beyond the fence surrounding their parental home. This happened, for instance, when their mothers went to the jungle for fire-wood or when both parents left for the market. Children usually cried briefly before somebody took care of them. Often they also stayed behind of their own accord at the community well, where they used to be 'entertained' by the girls and women fetching water early in the morning.

[54]Gell seems to use terms such as ancestors, spirits, ancestral spirits, ghosts, souls synonymously, and sometimes characterizes them as malicious or sacred, dangerous or protective. The transformation from the stage of a 'soul after death . . . to wander aimlessly' (Gell 1992: 37) to that of a 'sacred ancestor' (ibid.: 32) will probably take some time, but the reader is not informed about this process.

[55]*Bhat* is dying land that has been 'destroyed by swiddening and cultivation' (ibid.: 36). On a conceptual level it symbolizes any kind of problematic *transition*. Accordingly, the *bhat* also serves as the burial ground of the village, indicating that death is a transitory matter (as opposed to the concept of death as a singular event or point in time).

[56]For this reason remaining unmarried in Muria eyes is disastrous. The situation is similar in the case of an unmarried mother's illegitimate daughter, for example, from an illegitimate *ghotul* pregnancy, who will not be taken care of by or affiliated with the ancestral body of the mother's natal house.

the living either in their dreams or verbally through shamans in trance. The living, on the other hand, keep addressing and involving their ancestors in the course of the calendric festivals such as the first-fruit rituals and the life-cycle ceremonies of birth and marriage. In that way ancestors remain linked to societal issues of fertility, renewal and continuity. The cyclic aspect of tribal society is emphasized by ancestors staying close to their grandchildren in manifold ways: they are, for example, seen as quite physically involved in the protection of a child's sleep in his/her mother's womb (ibid.: 32) and in the naming ceremony or *satti* (ibid.: 32, 131) when they will ceremoniously leave the child's body and thereby contribute to affording the child with an individual name and social identity at the age of one month.

Gell characterizes M., the village, where she did fieldwork, as

> a singular, united entity whose finite boundaries are preserved and reflected in the upper world, where there is a heavenly counterpart of M. inhabited by gods born to the village, or married there according to affinal patterns that are analogous to those on earth, and ancestral spirits of departed M. souls. (ibid.: 71)

FIVE

Communicating with Their Ancestors: The Ho of Singhbum and Mayurbhanj

The Ho are a large tribe ethnically and linguistically linked to the Munda and the Santal, the Juang and the Sora.

In this chapter literature on the Ho that has not yet become part of the anthropological debate of Middle Indian tribal issues will be considered. Not all of the chosen material has been published. The focus of discussion is a critical assessment of the ethnography on the Ho of western Singhbum by Michael Yorke (1976 unpublished) complemented by the work of John Deeney, S.J. (1991, 2002[1975], 2005[1978].[1] Because of the focus of this chapter and in contrast to the previous chapter on the Hill Juang, Sora, Koya, and Muria Gond, a comparatively wider range of ethnographic background will be given in order to convey an ideational setting for the continued relationship of the Ho with their dead, an issue that both Yorke and Deeney have dealt with as a focal point of Ho culture and society. Additional material including Dhanur Singh Purty's publications (1978–82) on the Ho is given in the appendices.

According to the Census of India 2001 the Ho constitute 10.5 per cent of the total ST[2] population of Jharkhand or roughly

[1]Cf. Appendices 1 and 2.

One reason for the selection of this material on the Ho is personal: it was Deeney, who discussed central aspects of Ho culture with Yorke, for example the concept of *mandi chatu* (personal communication) and who introduced me to the Ho language.

[2]For a critical discussion of the official terms such as ST, SC, and OBC and the concept of Indian governmental pigeon-holing cf. Chapter Two.

744 142 people out of 7 087 068 of the state.[3] The official figures list the Ho as the fourth largest tribe in Jharkhand following the Santal, the Oraon and the Munda. It must be mentioned, though, that census figures with respect to particular tribes and tribal communities may not be reliable (Gell 1992: 1). Likewise, concerning Orissa figures for the Ho are not given in the Census of India 2001 although a considerable number of Ho are living there. It was in the northern tip of Mayurbhanj where I did fieldwork[4] in a Ho environment. There the border between Jharkhand and Orissa typically and arbitrarily cuts through the Kolhan, a 'compact' (Deeney 2002: ix) tribal territory of the Ho extending from West Singhbum eastwards into the neighbouring state.[5] Zimpel refers to the Ho as one of the largest Munda-speaking tribes in Bihar[6] and Orissa with a population of about 700 000 to 800 000; the number of Ho *speakers* may be about 1 million (Zimpel 2001: 212).[7] These figures reveal that Ho is spoken by a substantial number of people of non-Ho ethnicity living among the Ho, and using Ho as *lingua franca* (Deeney 2002: ix). Yorke makes the point that at the time of his fieldwork in the 1970s the 'Kolhan contains over half the Ho population,

[3]Jharkhand has altogether 30 STs, all of whom constitute 26.3 per cent of the total population of almost 27 million people.

[4]Cf. Prologue and Chapter One for details about my fieldwork.

[5]One of the weekly markets was held in Lagra on the Jharkhand side, and we regularly met villagers going there from Manbir.

[6]The southern half of Bihar became Jharkhand only in 2000.

[7]Deeney gives a similar number. According to the 1991 census (Part B: Language) there are 949 216 Ho speakers (Deeney 2005: iv), 653 429 in Bihar, 292 619 in Orissa. Interestingly, the Census of India (1991), Series 1: India, Part 1 of 1997, 'Language', gives figures concerning the *growth* of Ho below the heading 'Growth of Non-Scheduled Languages' as follows: 751 389 Ho speakers in 1971 become 783 301 speakers in 1981 and 949 216 in 1991. This indicates an increase of 4.25 per cent between 1971 and 1981 and a further increase of 21.18 per cent in the following ten years. If a similar increase has occurred since then, the topical number of Ho speakers today will clearly outnumber a million. However, as the absolute figures of the 2001 Census were not available to me, the last statement is speculative.

which is 250 000, with a further 200 000 scattered throughout Bihar and West Bengal' (Yorke 1976: 20).[8]

Linguistically the Ho language is classified as belonging to the Munda branch of the Austroasiatic language family[9] that comprises Indian tribal languages spoken by the Munda, Santal, Juang, and Sora, the Kharia, Bhil, Bondo, Gadaba, etc. (Deeney 2005: Introduction; Vitebsky 1993: 24) as well as languages spoken in Indonesia, Vietnam, Cambodia, Laos, and Myanmar. Moreover, Deeney in his *Ho Grammar and Vocabulary* gives examples of Oriya influence in Ho as different from Sadri influence in Munda (Deeney 2002: 135).

One of the specifics concerning the Ho system of social organization is its embeddedness in an outstandingly large number of clan or *kili* categories.[10] Deeney presents a list of 132 named clans or *kilis* of the Ho, not counting the sub-branches and without claiming completeness (ibid.). To each *kili* he indicates the respective 'brother' or *haga kilis* with whom marriages are not arranged.[11]

The alleged isolation of the Ho or the tribes of Middle India in general and their presumed lack of contact with Hindu India and its caste order for long periods in the past plays an important role not only in assessing future Ho prospects in terms of political, social and cultural transformation[12] but also in establishing a

[8]Yorke does not come up with the very source supporting this distribution of the Ho and reveals especially that almost 50 per cent of the overall population are supposed to live outside the Kolhan. Yorke's bibliography shows, however, that he has worked extensively through a number of Census reports and articles at Chaibasa and Ranchi University.

[9]For a more detailed, though tentative grouping of the languages of this family, see Deeney (2002: vii).

[10]This is quite different from the limited pattern of Santal clan categories.

[11]According to Deeney the system is slowly breaking down, so the 'purpose of listing these *haga kilis* is historical rather than social' (ibid.). This statement may be worth further anthropological investigation of Ho marriage patterns.

[12]Apart from Dumont's assessment of the tribes of India discussed in chapter 2, Yorke wonders if Ho society 'develop[ed] into a full caste system' (Yorke 1976: 52), should they come into greater contact with Hindu culture.

true picture of Ho culture in the course of history. 'There is a tremendous influence the Munda language family has had upon Sanskrit' (Pfeffer 1997: 5). Given this the possibility may be considered that 'tribal constructs of purity and pollution' (ibid.), for example, may have contributed to establishing the caste order of India—instead of the influence being the other way round, with Hindu 'immigrants', castes, and values leaving their imprint on tribal society in a kind of one-way traffic.

THE HO OF SARANDA

M. YORKE ON THE HO OF SINGHBUM: A CRITICAL INTRODUCTION INTO HIS THESIS

Yorke's doctoral thesis, 'Decision and Analogy: Political Structure and Discourse among the Ho Tribals of India', is based on sixteen months of fieldwork[13] in the Kolhan Government Estate of the Singhbum district (cf. Appendix 4). Between 1972 and 1974 he spent ten months among the Ho of Dubil, a village within the forested escarpment of the Saranda Hills.[14] Here the Ho have tried to make a living primarily as collectors of forest produce and also[15] as cultivators. Since this forested and hilly part of Singhbum does not yield sufficient land to be cleared and cultivated, most Ho are not able to live off their land exclusively. A few work in the nearby iron-ore mines, and wage-labour is a known fact in this environment containing rich mineral resources. Geographically this part of India belongs to the south-eastern extension of the Chota Nagpur Plateau, which is an area of uplands between the Gangetic and the Mahanadi

[13]Yorke spent three initial months in Chaibasa to study the language of the Ho as well as their history before he entered the field. At that time none of Deeney's three books on Ho language nor any of the seven booklets on Ho culture (Purty 1978–82) had been published.

[14]This is the hilly region in the south-west of Singhbum, where also R.O. Dhan (1961, 1962) conducted fieldwork.

[15]According to Zimpel the Ho fall into the category of 'settled agriculturalists' (Zimpel 2001: 212). This cannot be generalized, however, but it will hold true for Majumdar's Ho living in the plains of Singhbum (Majumdar 1950).

Plains, where the Ho live in permanent villages. Politically the Saranda Forest Area has become an administrative division in the southern part of Jharkhand, until 2000 southern Bihar. In anthropological terms the Ho ('/Munda and Kisan/Oraon clusters of tribal pairs' [Pfeffer 1997: 15]) culturally constitute part of what has been classified as *Chota Nagpur Complex* (ibid.: 19) and *Chota Nagpur Pattern* (ibid.: 15). Historically, according to Yorke (1976: 25), the Ho acknowledge the Bhuiya to be the original settlers of the area as much as they regularly make offerings to the Bhuiya goddess Paudi Ma whom they acknowledge as an 'attribute of their village guardian spirit' (ibid.: 27). Even after the Bhuiya have left the area, their main goddess is assumed as lingering around, and in numerous myths past relations between the Bhuiya and the Ho are kept alive.

Yorke's thesis is intended as a village study[16] focusing on the political and governmental activities of the village(rs) backed up by vivid case histories. In a second part Yorke analyses the communicative strategies applied in a particular dispute settlement at the village level to achieve a consensus between the conflicting parties involved.

Yorke's theoretical approach is structural-functionalist. In order to analyse the process of village government as set in the wider supralocal political environment, Yorke investigates the economic setting and the community structure of the village, land tenure and mortgage patterns, the Ho clan system and lineage structure, the special system of tribal administration, and the parallel *panchayat* system of 'regular'[17] administration. This local level

[16]Confining his focus to one village, Yorke cannot observe ties between villages. Only twice does he mention strong ties between Dubil and a neighbouring village 'in history and through marriage' (Yorke 1976: 207). Secondly, referring to pre-British times, he claims that 'the countryside was covered by a network of villages linked by affinal ties and by descent. . . . The village of Dubil is conscious of its links with three villages in the area where there are members of the same clan, all claiming common ancestors' (ibid.: 133). Marital rules and affinal links, however, are not explored in this thesis.

[17]Yorke's choice of words may be interpreted as implying that the native model is judged as irregular or 'anomalous' (Yorke 1976: 43). From the indigenous point of view this is obviously seen quite differently,

village 'government' under the hereditary authority of the village headman or *munda* is a key feature of Ho political organization, and it is in the recording of the ways of solving conflicts that matters of kinship and affinity, of ancestral protection, of Ho cosmology, of their spiritual world are revealed, negotiated and contested.

Yorke points out that he is mainly concerned with the 'secular aspect of the community' (Yorke 1976: 59), as he wants to understand 'political *behaviour* (my emphasis) and structure' (ibid.: 22). In fact, Yorke's interest in behavioural performances, in the manipulation of norms and in emotionally charged quarrels results in a number of detailed case histories, the presentation of which reveals that he has indeed been witness to a series of social dramas 'on the ground' and gained close inside knowledge. It is in the fascinating description, analysis and evaluation of the conflicting situations that the strength of his thesis lies.[18] These situations occur when consensual interaction between the quarrelling parties is no more possible on the 'non-public' or household level. Support on the village level becomes necessary

---

as tribal people label the official *panchayat* system as a *diku* (foreign, outsider) institution (Yorke 1976: 159).

This remark has been made because there are a few instances reflecting a certain ethnocentric stance. I will arbitrarily choose two or three more examples indicative of an (economic) bias. (1) Yorke claims that *individual entrepreneurship* faces difficulty in finding support from villagers (ibid.: 44), and (2) he concludes that 'it is necessary that more sources of wage employment become available to these forest villages' (ibid.: 43) or, in a different context, someone who can read and write, is labelled 'the most progressive of all' (ibid.: 205).

[18]The strength lies in unfolding conflicting processes up to a stage where they develop towards a state beyond 'private/individual' control. The other side of the coin is that Yorke tends to merge or confuse two different analytical levels: that of rules and norms and that of their deviations 'on the ground'. These violations of norms, which he documents precisely, lead him towards assuming a 'general blurring' (ibid.: 77) or 'fluidity' (ibid.: 207) of Ho *categories* (my emphasis), a 'flexibility of *norms* (my emphasis) governing *behaviour* (my emphasis)' (ibid.: 66). Instead, one might argue the other way round: the observed flexibility refers to the level of behavioural praxis 'on the ground' rather than to the level of the norms.

in order to restore the peace of the village and to also appease the village guardian spirit, who will get annoyed when village harmony is affected (cf. Sahlins 1968; Yorke 1976: 193).

However, isolating secular and religious matters as separate and unrelated categories and confining the focus of research to the secular sphere will constitute some sort of a problem when dealing anthropologically with a holistic society. (Tribal) ideas and values of seniority, of purity and pollution that pervade *all* of such a society are difficult to perceive, approach and assess when the overall ritual and ideological set-up is not taken into consideration, or if it is limited to its economic or political components or functions.[19] It was argued that in tribal societies 'egalitarianism is detected nowhere. Everywhere status differentiates two alike but unequal collectives' (Pfeffer 1997: 14). Hierarchical classification and ascribed senior/ junior status bears on (sub-)clan interrelationship, determines (rules of) marriageability[20] and on the whole constitutes the prerequisite and base of social and ritual interaction. But Yorke continuously conveys the portrayal of an egalitarian, non-hierarchical community (Yorke 1976: 38, 43, 46, 52, 64, 65, 77, 78, 85, 193). To Yorke there are two sources functioning as incentives to build up hierarchy. Firstly, hierarchy is the result of inequality which again is a matter of differences in wealth in terms of (cash) income, animals, land, other *economic* resources and

[19]Yorke is somewhat irritated, for instance, by the fact that 'wealthy people are only prepared to farm for their own household needs' thus missing out on economic possibilities of cash and profit-making (ibid.: 46). Without the ideological frame of reference Yorke does not seem able to understand a cultural logic in which any work *for others* is seen as polluting and degrading for tribal patrons, but not for their clients (Pfeffer 1997: 10).

[20]Yorke cuts a long story too short, when he writes about the relations between the Munda and the Ho: 'it appears quite clear that a rigid split has taken place as the two groups do not intermarry, even though many of the clans have the same name and both dialects are mutually comprehensible' (Yorke 1976: 130). This statement may be correct; however, it should be pointed out that *despite* the historical separation both Munda and Ho remain structurally related by the idiom of seniority within the 'fraternal relationship' classifying members of Ho clan categories as elder brothers and sisters.

political power.[21] Secondly, hierarchical classification to him is characteristic of Hindu caste society and synonymous with the interdependence of castes. As he correctly states that 'the structure of a Ho village is very different from the caste dominated village of the Hindu peasantry' (ibid.: 52), he wrongly concludes: It is 'largely egalitarian' (ibid.). As 'the distinctions of a *caste-like hierarchy* (my emphasis) tend to be forgotten' (ibid.: 78), hierarchy as such has ceased to exist.[22] When discussing marriage

[21]The title of Yorke's thesis contains the expression 'among the Ho Tribals of India'. He claims later, however, that the 'category of tribes has become a fiction or convention' (Yorke 1976: 32) as a result of the formation of the Jharkhand Party and the *panchayat* system, both instruments of political empowerment in a democratic India.

Confining the issue of tribe to its economic and political aspects, Yorke fails to gain access to the conceptual framework of tribal society, its ideological particularities such as the oppositional reckoning as basic principle of structuring Ho society, for instance, into marriageable and non-marriageable categories. Ho make a basic distinction between *haga* and *bala*. Seen from the perspective of any single clan, *haga* is a category of 'brothers' or 'one's *own* kin by birth' and as such not marriageable, *bala* is the category of 'kin by marriage' or affines. Yorke does not see this opposition between *haga* and *bala* as a key to understanding the system of Ho social organization and marriage rules. Instead, he treats *haga* as a *linguistic* category of inclusion denoting 'brother/comrade' when standing on its own or 'brotherliness' and 'brethrenship' when occurring in a compounded form. So he translates *hagakiliko* (*haga*: 'brother', *kili*: clan, *ko*: suffix indicating plural) wrongly as 'brethren of the clan' (ibid.: 200) instead of *'brother'* or *'sibling' clans* implying these are prohibited for intermarriage. In the same vein, he translates *hatuhagako* (*hatu*: village) as 'brethren of the village' (ibid.) and sees in this a statement of unity, harmony and reconciliation as opposed to a statement of disunity. I presume, however, this term denotes *'brother'/'sibling' village* and, as yet a speculation of mine, sparks off some idea of similarity to the Juang dualist division of marking whole villages as belonging to the non-marriageable *kutumb* half or the *bondhu* category. Just as the Bhuiya are considered senior to the junior Juang, the Bhuiya having settled in the Kolhan *before* the Ho, might be considered senior by these.

Interestingly, in the course of my fieldwork I have not come across the terms *hagakiliko* and *hatuhagako* (or I have not paid attention to them), but it might be worth while pursuing this in future fieldwork.

[22]In this Yorke is influenced by Bailey, whose concept of a 'caste-tribe continuum' he quotes (ibid.: 193).

restrictions between the 'dominant tribal section and the specialist groups' I think he refers to the localized lineages assigned to either of the categories of the landowner-patrons or the trader-clients. These categories are endogamous *vis-a-vis* each other and as such clearly not equal or interchangeable. He nevertheless confirms their egalitarian rather than hierarchical nature. 'Marriage restrictions between groups[23] are mainly reciprocal rather than hierarchical[24] and are not associated with a structure of economic subordination and domination. They . . . have no profound structural significance' (ibid.).[25]

As the reader's perception of Ho culture and society is shaped by Yorke's representation of it and also by his omissions, one more instance of criticism is given. There is a philosophy at work of (relative) ritual distinctions embedded, for example, in an institution called the *khunt,* a system of ascribed status differences and status categories 'crisscross[ing] the standard clan categories' (Pfeffer 1997: 19), alive 'in every village, every clan' (ibid.). This institution is missing in Yorke altogether.[26]

To conclude: anthropological key terms such as group, category, and clan are confused (Yorke 1976: 51, 52, 62, 66, 67, 70, 130, 159) just as principal differences between patrons and clients are either mixed up or remain vague (ibid.: 52, 68, 69, 71, 77).[27] Also, 'bridewealth' is consistently referred to as

[23]For the confusion of 'group' and 'category' see later in this section.

[24]If 'reciprocal' is opposed to 'hierarchical', 'reciprocal' seems to be equated with 'egalitarian/equal'. Hence the 'groups' involved are interpreted as equal to each other, their status distinctions ignored or abolished.

[25]Ignoring or negating the structural significance of the fundamental bifurcation of Ho society into marriageable or *bala* and not marriageable or *haga* categories is not a necessary consequence of the chosen structural-functionalist perspective, which was also applied by McDougal (1963).

Also, McDougal, for instance, spent a whole chapter on analysing Hill Juang *ritual* organization, thus highlighting its structural significance.

[26]He only once mentions the institution of a *khuntkatti* village as a 'traditional form of Munda village' (Yorke 1976: 129). Cf. Bauer on this issue with the Ho (Bauer 1987: 81).

[27]Referring to Majumdar (1950), Yorke speaks of land-owning and labouring *classes,* of *class* distinctions and preferential *class* endogamy. The problem is that neither of these terms (group, category, and class) is

'brideprice', although Yorke had collaborated with R.O. Dhan, who is quite explicit in this point arguing against the notion of 'buying a bride' as reflected in the term 'brideprice' and enlarging on the social web of ties brought about by the intricate mechanism of the distribution of 'bridewealth' or *gonong* in the same area of research as Yorke (cf. Dhan 1961: 68).

THE SETTING OF YORKE'S FIELDWORK: LOCAL AND SOCIAL

Dubil is a multi-clan village containing local lineages assigned to different Ho and Santal[28] clans who co-reside economically independent of each other. The relations between the households as basic corporate units are structured on lineage and landholding patterns. In the village, a fairly recent settlement founded about four generations ago, live also members of 'servicing castes' or 'specialist groups' (Yorke 1976: 52). The Ho are the dominant tribal section, yet the relation between Ho and Santal is said to be 'not hierarchical' (ibid.: 64). Yorke describes Ho social organization as based on a 'rudimentary segmentary model' (ibid.: 50) determined by descent, kinship, and land tenure. Time and again Yorke discusses in some depth issues of inheritance and corporate landownership, of mortgage procedures and of disputes over rights of cultivation. By law, land is protected for the tribal people. It can neither be sold to anyone outside the village nor to anyone who is a non-tribal. Yorke stresses the importance of the village and of the households, set within the web of local lineages or sub-clans as points of reference and identification for every Ho and the fundamental social units rather than the culturally distant category of the tribe (cf. Sahlins 1968: 16). The village is a sphere of culture as opposed to that of the wild outside forest, an area beyond human control. The village also houses Ho ancestors within its

---

clearly defined and that they are used almost synonymously. Similarly, the landowners' *clients* are referred to as an 'unspecified class of landless labourers' (Yorke 1976: 22).

[28]The Santal clans are Murmu and Hansda, according to Pfeffer (2002d: 71) hierarchically the two most superior.

boundaries. According to their myth of origin the villagers conceive of themselves as living within a 'religiously defined boundary that is realised through a contract with the village guardian spirit' (Yorke 1976: 55) or *hatubonga* who acts as a protective agent residing in the heart of every Ho village in a sacred grove or *sarna*.[29] On the other hand, Ho feel threatened by the forest spirits or *burubongako* and other spirits.

Within the village as an environment of uncentralized political structure, moral authority is entrusted in the village priest or *diuri* performing as the sacred leader of the village and the village headman or *munda* who is the secular leader. He for his part finds himself under the ultimate authority of the paramount headman or *manki,* who has responsibilities on a supra-village level.

HO ANCESTORS IN THE WORLD OF THE LIVING

In Yorke's thesis the reader learns comparatively little about processes of transition and transformation that a dead Ho may be subject to after his physical death. This remark is made bearing in mind what van Gennep, Bloch and Hertz had to say, and how Vitebsky and Demmer, for example, illustrated this issue ethnographically. Due to a focus on secular matters, no analysis of the pantheon of the Ho spirit world is given, and the conceptual differences between ancestors, spirits, ancestral spirits, ancestry, soul, shade, and *bonga* remain vague.

However, as will have been assumed, it is impossible to enlarge on the world of the living excluding their interrelation with the dead. In fact, Yorke convincingly implies the idea that the intersection and focal point of the living and the dead is embedded in Ho notions of kinship and (ancestral) land. Of the many instances in Yorke's thesis a few have been chosen which reveal

[29]In the Ho villages that I have been to the sacred grove was always outside the village boundaries and called *desauli*. This was so in Lupungutu near Chaibasa in Jharkhand and in a number of villages in the north of Mayurbhanj. According to Deeney (3/unpubl.) Ho do not use the term *sarna*, but the Santal do. Interestingly, in Yorke's site of fieldwork there were two Santal local lineages co-residing with the Ho.

that contrary to how Sora ancestors were depicted as interfering agencies, Ho ancestors are involved in the everyday lives of their descendants rather than involving themselves actively.[30]

(1) *Ancestors, Lineage and Land*

The local lineage is initially established by the original ancestor who either founded the village or cleared land in the village. It is the local group of the clan or *kili*, consisting of all the 'descendants in the patrilineal line of a known or fictitious common ancestor' (ibid.: 87). The unity of the local lineage is expressed in terms of rights over common land which is ancestral land. The possible alienation of lineage or ancestral land must be prevented under any circumstances.[31] A lineage's common ownership of land and its common ancestry are conceptually interrelated to the effect that the category of the ancestors provides the very precondition and base of their descendants' existence. For this support and protection, ancestors are ritually taken care of, verbally addressed, and regularly given offerings of rice-beer and meat.

By providing and passing on land, ancestors are symbols of (a lineage's) unity and continuity.

(2) *Ancestors and 'Adin'*

The soul or *rowa:* of a deceased person is kept in the *adin*, an inner room and the sacred part of the Ho house, where the

[30]It goes without saying that this may also be the result of Yorke's representation of Ho ancestry.

[31]Yorke gives an example in this context which shows—contrary to what he is saying elsewhere—how facts 'on the ground' are manipulated and rearranged to make them coincide with tribal values of land-tenure and kinship norms: A man who has no sons may arrange an uxorilocal marriage for his daughter. His daughter's husband will not change his clan for that matter, but he will temporarily hold his wife's father's land for his wife's father's grand-children, i.e. his own sons. These will be taken into the clan of their mother's father, not their father. Thereby the grandfather's lineage will not be discontinued and the ancestral land is kept within the lineage (ibid.: 95–6).

family meal is prepared. This is an area of purity where the ancestors of the patrilineage or *owa: goe:* (the dead of the house) are assumed to dwell and where they are venerated. It might be argued (although Yorke does not say so) that as a woman after marriage becomes a member of her husband's *kili* and adopts her husband's lineage's ancestors, she will after her death also become entitled to ancestor veneration within her husband's *adin*. After all, after marriage she is no more allowed to enter her natal or paternal *adin*.[32]

Temporarily, in times of trouble and illness, affinal *hortenko*[33] as a second category of ancestors are believed to also stay there. This category includes 'the spirits of all the dead women of the lineage, i.e. the mothers and paternal grandmothers' (Yorke 1976: 93), also the ancestors of the 'mother's patrilineage, the wife's patrilineage and the sister's husband's patrilineage' (ibid.). As ancestors they are integrally in charge of protecting the well-being of the household: its members, its land, its harvest, and its cattle.

(3) *Ancestors and Fertility*

In Dubil, the village where Yorke conducted fieldwork, the original settlers' goddess Paudi Ma is worshipped, an act that is considered necessary for the growth of the dry rice crop.[34] Being female the topic of fertility is implied. Also, in Dubil, Paudi Ma is addressed as the 'main consort of the village guardian spirit'

[32]Dhan (1961: 60–1) is very clear on this: 'A woman after her death becomes an ancestor of her husband's kili and she will not be remembered by her paternal kinsmen in her natal village.'

[33]Both terms are not included in the Ho-English Dictionary (Deeney 2005) as compounds. To make a distinction between one's own and one's affinal ancestors would make sense, however, within the cultural logic of tribal values, since the world of the dead is modelled on the world of the living (Sahlins 1968).

[34]This has been interpreted as expressing the tribal idea of the goddess who is conceived as the landowner. Provided with an offering, she will then provide fertility to the soil in a divine gift-exchange (cf. Pfeffer 1997: 9).

(ibid.: 55). The case of a Bhuiya goddess in a cultural Ho context reveals a broad supra-tribal understanding of ancestry.

(4) *Ancestors and Graveyard*[35]

A socially complete person is a member of both local lineage and village. By passing on their name in the naming ceremony, ancestors contribute to a new born baby acquiring membership in the local lineage. Membership of the village is ascribed by birth into the local lineage expressing a ritually important step of the transformation into a Ho *person*. It is by the establishment of the graveyard of the local lineage within the village boundaries, usually under the shade of a large tree at the centre of the fields of the local lineage, that 'full membership of a village . . . is sealed' (Yorke 1976: 86). According to Yorke, those members of the local lineage, who 'bury their dead in the same graveyard and therefore live in the same village' (ibid.: 89) are also those who are involved in the funeral ceremony.[36] It is assumed that the grave contains the bodily substance, the biological element of the deceased, whereas his soul or shadow, *rowa* or *umbul*,[37]

[35]Interestingly, there is no entry for 'graveyard', 'cemetery' or 'burial ground' in Deeney (2005: 145; [1975]2002: 150, 160), but for 'grave' or *hasa huwan* (*hasa*: earth, soil; *huwan*: ravine, deep pit), 'burial place' or *sasan* and 'burial stone or *sasan diri* (put flat over the grave); *biddiri* (a standing memorial stone)'.

[36]This would imply that lineage members or affines from other villages are not included in the funeral ceremony, which would run contrary to what I could observe among the Ho and to what McDougal (1963), Vitebsky (1993), and Demmer (2007) had to say on the Hill Juang, Sora and Koya. It would also run contrary to what Yorke himself said about the significance of the mother's brother or *mamu* (Yorke 1976: 94) who would probably live outside the village. I find it hard to imagine that the *mamu* plays an important role in arranging the marriage of his sister's son, but not in the funeral ceremony. Also, Bauer (1987) points to the presence of the MB (mother brother) as obligatory in the literature that she studied.

[37]Yorke speaks of three elements that constitute a Ho person (Yorke 1976: 102): (1) the breath of life or *jibon*, (2) the bodily substance or *jangjilu* (*jang*: bone, *jilu*: flesh), and (3) the soul or character or *umbul*. *Jilu* is that part that is 'returned to the earth that was cleared by the common ancestor of the local lineage, thus again stressing the association of blood and land.' (ibid.)

is called back and will reside inside the house or *adin*. A large slab of stone or *sasan diri*[38] is placed horizontally over the grave immediately after the burial.

It is due to an ancestor, i.e. after having settled in a village for at least one generation, that a local lineage may establish their graveyard and thereby obtain and secure their permanent right of residence. It is the village council who has to grant the request for a burial site, and the local lineage demanding that site has to give a feast for the whole village in return. The grave in this respect reflects and expresses cosmological aspects of place and time, of identity and continuity, and reveals the social nature of dealing with death.

(5) *Ancestors and 'Mandi Chaturenko'*

The earthen pot used for cooking rice is called *mandi chatu*. To avoid it from being polluted by 'evil eyes', it is usually kept inside the *adin*, the cooking hearth and ancestral abode. As a metaphor of the unity of the local lineage which is Yorke's interpretation, it turns into (*miyad*) *mandi chaturenko* or 'people of one rice pot' (Yorke 1976: 87). In the case of death the rice pot of the deceased's household should be broken in the same way as 'all the households of the local lineage must throw out their rice pots and get a new one' (ibid.: 89). In this new pot the spirit of the deceased is finally invited to stay as an ancestor and it is here where s/he will be venerated.

Deeney broadens this somewhat limited village perspective of local lineage ancestry by referring the concept of *mandi chaturenko*[39] to

[38]Chosen and carried by those of the deceased's local lineage 'who can attend' (ibid.: 102).

This part of preparing the burial was a lengthy affair of a complete day, *obligatory* for each household of the village to be represented by at least one male member, in Manbir, fixed on the third day after the immediate burial of the body itself and sparking off a series of ritual performances in the course of the following days.

[39]A concrete illustration from my fieldwork is given in Appendix 3.

all those descended from a common ancestor, from people who once ate from the same pot. This is reckoned as far back as people can remember, e.g. 4 or 5 generations. All these[40] may enter one another's *adin*, and should anyone of these die, all the others must remove from service the *mandi chatu* then in use. (Deeney 2005: 242)

In other words, several generations of bilateral kin beyond the local lineage acknowledge the same set of ancestors who are collectively remembered in manifold places and represented in each household by the *mandi chatu*. Women marrying virilocally will become members of their husbands' lineages. Wives will also adopt the ancestors of their husbands' patrilineages. This is a ritually and socially important step in a Ho woman's process of transformation.

Yorke and Deeney have related the institution of the *mandi chaturenko* to Ho notions of purity and descent, whereas by including the idea of commensality it has also been interpreted as a Ho concept of constructing kinship and affinity, or rules of (non-)marriageability for the cognates of three generations.[41]

Yorke had directed his focus towards the secular sphere. However, despite this intention we can see how integrally rooted Ho ancestors are in the social cosmos of every Ho at the household level, the village level and beyond. Ho ancestors seem to be a social fact that cannot be isolated as a separate, unrelated category.

ANCESTORS, LIFE-CYCLE AND THE LANGUAGE OF ANCESTOR VENERATION

In a number of unpublished papers J. Deeney (cf. Appendices 1 and 2) has dealt with the Hos' continued communication with their dead and the entwinement of ancestors, spirits and *bongas*

[40]This is clearly more differentiated than Yorke's statement that 'kin *and villagers* (my emphasis)' are allowed to enter the *adin* (ibid.: 87).

[41]Cf. Pfeffer (1997: 24; ibid. 2002b: 223). The importance of the discrepancy as regards the depth of three, four, or five generations as given by Deeney and Pfeffer may be worth further investigation. Cf. Appendix 3 for the *mandi chaturenko* of my *saki*.

in the spirit world (Deeney: 1-3/unpublished and Deeney n.d.).[42] These articles have been written by someone who is not an anthropologist, but has dedicated his life to exploring Ho culture and language and lived among the Ho for more than half a century.

ANCESTORS AND LIFE-CYCLE

Childbirth is considered a period of impurity for all those who are immediately involved in the process of delivery, which includes in the case of the Ho the husband who functions as midwife. Deeney claims this is a unique Ho institution which to his knowledge is neither shared by the Munda nor the Santal nor any other tribal group.[43] Impurity results in touching taboos and taboos of commensality for a preliminary period of up to one month. Since impurity is interpreted as contagious quality, those attached to the new born baby and its impure state are conceived as potentially dangerous to the ancestors and the village.[44] The sacred part of the house or *adin* may not be entered. Only after a number of purifying rituals addressed to the ancestors to make good for the impurity they have been exposed to is the baby introduced to them. Transformed into a social being or person, the new born child becomes entitled to ancestral protection and intercession. This process is completed by the naming ceremony.

The role of the ancestors clearly reveals their conceptual involvement from the very first moment of an individual's biological existence after childbirth, and in the process of the

[42]Deeney made these articles available to me in 2006 and agreed to my making use of them, for which I am very grateful. Deeney (3/unpubl.) has been revised, enlarged and published (Deeney 2008).

[43]My Santal assistant, who has lived with Ho people for more than twenty years, had not even heard of this institution.

[44]It had been argued in Chapter 3 (concering the concept of the person in holistic societies) that human qualities and relations are not classified into those of a primary and those of a secondary order of minor significance. Likewise the impurity of members of a household is considered real and material, a social fact not only expressing something, but also doing or causing something.

baby's transformation into a social being. Seen from the perspective of the new born child this 'enters into a relationship not only with the living but also with the dead members of the family' (Deeney 2/unpubl.: 2).

Likewise in rituals such as the *jom isin* ceremony, a wife is introduced to the ancestors of her husband's patrilineage, just as they are introduced to her. Before this ritual has been completed she will not be allowed to enter her husband's *adin*, touch the rice pot or *mandi chatu* or prepare the 'family' meal there. Structurally similar to a person's transformation around childbirth, a wife enters into a relationship not only with her husband but also with his ancestors.

ANCESTOR VENERATION

For Deeney the term *worship* connotes 'adoration shown to a deity' (Deeney 3/unpubl.: 26). For this reason he prefers to speak of ancestor *veneration* instead of ancestor worship, since with the Ho ancestors, although they are assumed to have passed over into the invisible spirit world, are in no way considered to be divine. On the contrary, they retain human qualities, inclinations and defects analogous to those that they had when alive.[45]

Persons eligible for veneration as ancestors are those whose soul or *rowa* is eligible to be called into the *adin* after death. This holds basically true for every Ho except (a) those who die a violent death, e.g. from a tiger, or small pox and other infectious diseases, (b) women who die in childbirth before giving birth to

[45]Deeney gives a vivid example in this context, referring to the Encyclopedia Mundarica (Hoffmann, J. ed. 1950: 1640) and indicating that the Munda seem to classify their ancestors similarly.

On the occasion of the *hero: porob* feast (cf. Appendix 2, Book 2) each Ho household sacrifices a goat, a ritual which is performed in a field. Eventually the head of the family makes an offering of the meat, rice, and rice-beer to the ancestors at the site of the sacrifice in the field. Before having his own meal there, 'he goes to his house, enters the *adin* and there makes another offering to those dead ancestors who due to physical disabilities, lameness, blindness, or the like, were unable to attend the sacrifice in the field' (Deeney n.d.: 5).

the child, (c) those who have been outcast either because of marrying too close, e.g. within the same *kili* which is considered incest, or because of marrying a non-Ho,[46] and (d) children who die before the naming ceremony.[47]

Ancestor veneration is expressed at the village level on the occasion of the village festivals, and the 'family' level.[49] Deeney points out that at the village level (cf. Appendix 2: Festivals or *Porobko*) the ancestors of about two previous generations are addressed,[49] whereas at the 'family' level all descendants of a common ancestor about four or five generations back would be called by name. This will usually involve fifteen to twenty agnates patrilineally related within the same (sub-)clan or *kili*.[50] Inside the *adin*, the male head of the household in his priestly function will call out the names of these ancestors and make offerings of meat, cooked rice, and rice-beer.[51] In spite of spatially separate

[46]In Manbir I took down the pedigree of Giridari Bage of the dominant founding clan. His FZeH (father's elder sister's husband) or *mamu* was a non-Ho, and further information concerning his children was refused. The same applied to his DyH (younger daughter's husband) a non-Ho from Bubaneshwar. Thus outcasting someone implies a mental dimension well beyond the act of cutting social ties.

[47]In Pathan Sai during my fieldwork the village priest's or *diuri's* new-born baby had lived through the shaving ceremony successfully (Day 9 after birth), but died before the naming ceremony to be performed on the 21st day. Consequently it was buried somewhere outside the village.

[48]Deeney does not resort to anthropological kinship jargon, but applies terms such as 'family', 'direct relatives', 'sister/brother in a very broad sense', etc. When dealing with his work, I will use his terms in inverted commas.

[49]Amounting to more than 126 names which the village priest or *diuri* addresses in one example that Deeney gives from a tape recording on the occasion of rites performed prior to *mage porob*.

[50]Cf. Appendix 3 which gives the names of 26 ancestors constituting *the mandi chaturenko* of my *saki's* from Pathan Sai. 'Women and children, although included among the ancestors being venerated, would not be named' (Deeneey n.d.: 6). Maternal kin is excluded, since they do not belong to the same clan category.

[51]Where I conducted fieldwork *everybody* I met, including very young children, gave three drops of whatever they were about to drink, rice-beer or water, to the floor before they would start eating.

adins belonging to the households of the local lineages at the village level and beyond, the same set of ancestors will be simultaneously venerated in all the *adins* of those related as *miyad mandi chaturenko*.

The Language of Ancestor Veneration

On different occasions Ho ancestors are addressed differently:

(1) Deeney shows that female ancestors are included, though not named, in ancestor veneration. For instance, on the vigil of the village flower feast or *ba porob* (cf. Appendix 2: Book 2) a standard(ized) way of addressing the ancestors is: 'Listen, you old men and old women, mothers and fathers.'[52]

(2) Ho use the term *ham hoko* (old men) to designate male ancestors, mostly followed by the parallel *dum hoko* (sleeping men). Ho do not refer to their ancestors as *bongas* or spirits but as continued 'family' members who have entered the invisible spirit world of *Sinbonga* and the *bongas*.

(3) Close relations among ancestors of the same *kili* are assumed to exist analogous to those among the living: 'you all sit together on the same stool' or 'you are closely united (stretched out hand in hand, arm in arm) as are the teeth of a bear-trap'.[53]

(4) Ancestors are attributed agency and intercessory power with the *bongas* and *Sinbonga*, when these are urged to ask for favours on behalf of the living. Terms such as 'say to him' and 'tell him' (*kajiyaipe*) occur regularly.

(5) In Ho there are two ways of expressing 'we', the personal pronoun in the first person plural:[54] (a) *abu* including the person(s) addressed, and (b) the excluding *ale*. When addressing their ancestors Ho often use the inclusive forms, e.g. in the *keya ader* ritual, in which the soul or *rowa* is

[52]'*Ocho ape hamko buriko, engako apuko.*'

[53]'*miyad gandu miyad charpare dubakan jaruwakante*', or '*ratamleka-paseleka ti:yakan-gatiyakante, norakan-jangiyakante*' (Deeney n.d.: 7).

[54]For the respective possessive pronoun 'our' or *abuwa*: cf. Prologue.

called inside the *adin*: 'Let *us* go to *our* house.' (*Abuwa: duwartebu seno:wa*).

(6) In the same ceremony ancestors are asked to 'bring back *our* dead brother/sister to *our* house. From today unite him/her to yourselves. He/she is *our* brother/sister.'[55]

These examples may indicate the Ho ancestors' ambiguous state. On the one hand they are continuously treated as members of the household and as remaining part of the world of the living; on the other hand they are seen to have acquired a special status as members of the spirit world due to their potential access to *Sinbonga*. Both views reflect the Hos' continued interaction with their ancestors which is clearly reflected in the language of veneration.

THE HOS' SPIRIT WORLD

Deeney translates *Sinbonga* as God.[56] Ho often address him as king or *raja*. He is conceived as the supreme creator, an attribute that belongs uniquely to him. All other spirits are subject to him. To some of them Sinbonga has given a role in protecting men. Shamans, too, rely and depend on Sinbonga, calling him the 'guru of their gurus'. His creating capacity is synonymous with his generative power from which everything has been propagated, including men, rice or *baba* and other plants, cattle, silkworms and other animals, all referred to by the generic term 'seeds' or *hita*. Seeds connote the idea of growth and the capacity to generate more of one's kind. Likewise, in the compounds 'rice-mother' or *baba enga* (or 'goat-mother' or 'silkworm-mother' or 'millet- mother', etc.) Sinbonga's 'creative energy communicated to [plants and] creatures in different spheres' (Deeney 3/unpubl.: 29) is personified in the notion of 'mother'

[55]'*Abuwa: haga-misi goeyani: adeyani: . . . abuwa: owa: duwartege agu-ura-i-pe, tisinete gati-misa-i kili-misa-i-pe . . . niyo abuwa: haga-misi-tangeyae:*' (ibid.).

[56]In prayers of a Ho congregation at a catholic mass held in Ho, God will be addressed as Sinbonga (cf. also Appendix 1). Most of this paragraph refers to an essay of about 40 pages by Deeney (3/unpubl. on 'The Hos' Spirit World'.

stressing fecundity and generations to come. Accordingly, Sinbonga is addressed: 'you have created', 'you have given life', 'you have given growth', 'you have given increase', 'you have provided men with a world in which to dwell' (ibid.: 2). An offering made to Sinbonga is always an animal of a white colour, and vice versa animals of a white colour are offered only to him.

Spirits or *bongako* are classified as tutelary as well as malign categories of named spirits. The term *bonga* relates to the 'disembodied spirit of a dead human being and therefore a *bonga*' (ibid.: 27).[57] *Bongas* are also believed to have been created in order to involve themselves in the lives of men, for example at the time of the rice harvest, in times of sickness, when making promises, in the course of life-cycle rituals, when going to the jungle, etc. The generic term for the category of protective spirits is *ma:-nam chalu:-nam bongako*, i.e. those who have revealed themselves in the process of clearing the jungle (*chalu*: to hoe). Often Ho consider these spirits to be more directly involved in their lives than Sinbonga himself. The principal yearly feasts in which the village priest or *diuri* presides in the name of the whole village, such as *mage, ba*, and *batauli* (cf. Appendix 2/Book 2) are addressed to the tutelary spirits. Desauli figures prominently as the village guardian spirit and the spirit of the holy grove, whereas Jayer Buri is considered to be his wife and a generative force of obvious connotations of fecundity and fertility reflected in the obscene language used in the course of the *mage* feast. Desauli and Jayer Buri are complemented by *maran bonga* and a complex pantheon of more named *bongas*, female and male, who, including their servicing *bongas,* populate mountains, hills, streams, fields, trees, springs, and deep water pools, thus constructing spatial categories and rooting the world of the *bongas* in the landscape of the living.

[57]Deeney refers to the Sre and Jarai of Vietnam, who speak a Mon-Khmer language. They use the term *böngat* denoting 'the shadow or spiritual double of a human being', which may connote the word *umbul*, 'the primary meaning of which is shadow, but which is also used to refer to the disembodied *rowa* of a dead person' (Deeney 3/unpubl.: 27).

Malign spirits are responsible for epidemics and diseases to men, cattle, and crops. They sometimes act in collaboration with men, trying to inflict harm upon someone else. Deeney says that there is a clear association of these harmful spirits with the Hindu goddess Kali.[58] Belief in malicious spirits is obviously widespread and Purty has paid as much attention to them as to the tutelary spirits (Purty 1978–82). Malign spirits fall under the jurisdiction of the shamans and never under that of the village priest or the head of the household in his priestly role. When they require sacrifices these are 'never made with any dispositions of respect or with any intention of showing honour to the spirit, but it is a kind of bribe to get rid of the spirit' (Deeney 3/unpubl.: 33).

Most *bongas*, including the category of the spatial ones, may conceptually be understood as the spirits of dead persons as unfolded in the Asur legend (cf. Appendix 2). This legend known to both Munda and Ho, establishes in myth a basis for considering the *bongas* of the hills, rivers, etc., to be the spirits of the dead Asur widows.

Concluding from the work of Yorke and Deeney on the Ho, the relation between the living and the dead reveals that ancestors are integrally involved in Ho social and ritual life. They are characterized as beneficial if served properly. The concept of the Ho person, as vaguely as it has been delineated by Yorke, seems to revolve around ancestors as a constitutive factor. In Yorke's thesis as well as in those texts by Deeney that were accessible, ancestors provide focus and orientation and are a given social and ritual fact. What may be interesting to establish more clearly in future fieldwork is the making of or turning into an ancestor and the transformational phases after death as opposed to being a (static) ancestor. What are the processes of transition of soul, body and mourners? What is the dangerous potential implied in the social impurity of death, in the liminal stage of the 'soul'? Is there a notion of a risky and lengthy journey of the soul, only eventually growing to become a benevolent ancestor, and how

[58]He makes this statement after having gone into the etymology of the names of her servicing spirits and into the sacrificial formulas.

do the living manage to cope with this? Is there is also the tripartite structure that van Gennep had made out in rituals, including death rituals?[59]

An example given by Yorke highlights the conceptual value attached to Ho ancestors by the living. In the course of a conflict a father in his rage had burnt down his son's house; according to the villagers his son had been murdered that way. The argument was that by burning the house the *adin* and the ancestral spirits had also been destroyed. And as nobody could survive without his ancestral protection, the son was considered dead, although he was clearly seen as being physically alive.

Yorke claims that kinship, ancestors and land may be considered separate analytic categories, but for the Ho they are 'different aspects of the same reality' (Yorke 1976: 126) and conceptually interrelated, a statement with which Deeney would surely agree. The living and the dead live close to each other in Ho society: agnatic ancestors are assigned the sacred part of the house, the *adin*, and are thereby attributed superior status. They

[59]I gained some idea of this when I witnessed burial ceremonies in the course of my fieldwork. In some instances a temporal structure of three phases was clearly present: after the immediate burial of the body on the day of death, phase 1/day 1 began with a ritual called *rowa agu* or guiding the soul from the grave to the house, followed on the second day by *rowa dili* or taking the soul with the help of a straw, some cotton, and a hoe to a pond and fixing an *uneven* number of 3, 5, 7, 9, or 11 days for the next phase to take place. Phase 2 would consist of 4 days (day 1: for men getting the burial stone or *sasan diri* from the jungle, for women to produce leaf cups and leaf plates; day 2: purifying rituals or *sabsi* consisting of taking a ritual bath and, separate for men, a shaving ceremony, and, for women, putting on new cloths; for both and the complete funeral party, the earth ritural; day 3: (a) ritual against evil spirits, the evil eye, any kinds of danger or *ere bonga;* (b) calling the soul into the *adin* or *umbul ader/ keya ader* with the MB (Mother Brother) as the head of the ritual; (c) ritual on the threshing ground (for men only) or *kolam bonga;* day 4: *adin bonga* or integration ritual. After another break of several days, weeks, months, or sometimes a year or more phase 3 would consist of up to three days of a second burial or *diri dulsunum,* in the course of which *balas* (affines) and *hagas* (agnatic group) would meet, celebrate (*jomnu*: eat and drink), dance, and pour (*dul*) oil (*sunum*) on the burial stone (*diri*).

symbolize fertility, growth, land, continuity, unity, and protection; in case malicious ancestral agency is identified, there are known ways of investigation and ritual treatment. Ho ancestors and spirits are simultaneously members of the 'family'. As such they are mediating between the world of the living and the world of the dead.

Plate 1: Death ritual at Gara Sai, Mayurbhanj, Orissa. After the burial of the body the 'soul' is offered rice, water, and a tooth brush (Sunday, 8 January 2006, 8.32 a.m.).

Plate 2: Death ritual at Gara Sai, Mayurbhanj, Orissa. Purification ritual or *sabsi*. Attached to the deceased's hoe, his 'soul' has been placed in a pond for 9 days (Sunday, 8 January 2006, 10.31 a.m.).

Plate 3: Death ritual at Gara Sai, Mayurbhanj, Orissa. After a ritual bath the widow and her helpers guide the 'soul' home (Sunday, 8 January 2006, 10.32 a.m.).

SIX

Conclusion

Of the four different 'tribal zones' (Pfeffer 1997: 6) of the Indian subcontinent, the focus in this paper has been on that of Middle India, in particular on a limited number of tribal societies living in central-eastern India in what is divided into the modern-day states of Orissa, Chhattisgarh and Jharkhand. Extending over a distance of some 700 km from the river Godavari in the south towards the Chota Nagpur plateau of Jharkhand in north-easterly direction, the hilly and mountainous countryside and the plateaux to the west of the Eastern Ghats are the region of those who refer to themselves as 'humans' in their respective languages. By outsiders they are given a variety of 'invented terms' (Gell 1992: 2), which they never or hardly ever use themselves such as Muria, Maria, Gond, Koya, Sora, Kond, Bhuiya, Juang, Ho, Munda, Kharia, Oraon.

Demmer's Koya or Bison Horn Maria settle in Malkangiri, the southernmost tip of Orissa neighbouring Gell's Muria Gond of Bastar (in the state of Chhattisgarh to the west) with whom they are linguistically related as speakers of Dravidian languages. In a cultural perspective beyond the language the Gondide Koya in the south and the Ho and Munda in the north are said to be related by a common tradition of megalithic funerary rituals (cf. Pfeffer 2002d: 66). Further north-east, as seen from Malkangiri, we find Vitebsky's Lanjia Sora. They are related to McDougal's Hill Juang of Keonjhar in northern Orissa, both speaking languages of the Munda branch of the Austroasiatic language family. Bhuiya and Hill Juang are neighbours of Deeney and Yorke's Ho (and Santal), living just across the state border to the north in Singhbum (Jharkhand) and also east in Mayurbhanj (north-east Orissa). Ho, Santal, Sora, and Hill Juang are interrelated by being members of the same language family.[1]

Monographs and articles on the Hill Juang, Sora, Koya, Muria Gond and Ho have been studied in this volume, the criterion for selection being mainly the authors' expertise and open-mindedness to perceive and convey the richness of the cultures in which they did extended fieldwork. Their publications serve as mind-openers for those who are interested in 'particular form[s] of humanity' (Dumont 1986: 205–6), the plural form indicating the wide range of cultural variations that an anthropologist will be confronted with in the tribal societies of Middle India. The ethnographic material discussed and compared in this study may serve as a quarry for future research into the workings of the 'savage minds'—the plural forms this time owed to caution about unwarranted generalizations. The 'savage mind' in anthropological terms denotes an 'option of the human mind'[2] (cf. chapter 3). However, until today it is judged by both the Indian Government and the Ministry of Tribal Affairs as the backward mind (without inverted commas and without self-consciousness) of those '[tribes] of whom some are still adhering to their primitive culture and abstaining the shadows of modernization'.[3] The controversy about tribal societies' neglect and distortion in anthropology has been dealt with parallel with that of the governmental policy of 'uplifting'.

Quite on the contrary, Gell characterizes the Muria as 'bursting with confidence in the rightness of their way of doing things' (Gell 1992: 17). This is a statement that may hold true for all or most of the other tribes as well. However, this 'bursting with confidence' is not to be understood as an intrapersonal psychological feature but has a strong social quality about it—as has the 'bursting into tears' in the case of death and grieving that conveys a spirit of dignity, outspokenness, and clarity to the

[1]For a more precise and at the same time tentative grouping of the languages cf. Deeney (2002: Introduction).

[2]This idiom coined by Lévi-Strauss and its implications are discussed by Petermann (2004: 866).

[3]www.orissagov.nic.in/census, link: Orissa Human Development Report/ Introduction (23.06.2007).

mourners, so markedly different from the display of awkwardness and helplessness in other societies. The Ho whom I have met, young and old, female and male, radiate this quality out to others, also in their grieving. They act as *dividuums* and members of a 'whole society' embedded in a universal order which permeates the entire cosmos.[4] Perhaps the public expression of this 'oneness' with the cosmos in tribal societies, in which death, the living and the dead are integrally included in a, basically, social world, comes very close to that 'dream of wholeness, the vision of a world whose meaning is contained within itself, of a life that is complete, of a place where all things touch' (Trawick 1992: xvii).[5]

Much in the same matter-of-fact way that kin and affines are excluded in Western ways of dealing with death, they are included in known, differentiated, non-individual and structured ways in the tribal societies of Middle India. Instances of this were discussed in Chapters Four and Five, reflecting how the meanings of deaths (and lives) are negotiated and contested. If death is conceived of as a phoneme, its meaning cannot be revealed by looking at it in isolation. It obtains its meaning by its being related to other societal phonemes such as tribal society's social organization, its ritual, its pantheon of gods, goddesses, and spirits, and its ancestors. It is felt that the ethnographic material discussed in this study has contributed in profound and sensitive ways to coming to terms with culturally specific notions of life by focusing on the dead and the issue of death in tribal societies.

In this vein it has also contributed to 'the purpose of anthropology [which is] to make the world safe for human differences. (Ruth Benedict).[6]

[4]Vitebsky focused on this complex of 'public procedures and supposed inner feelings' being linked in the Sora funeral sequence (1993: 237).

[5]Trawick's quotation was given at the end of Chapter One as a mental note and an overall frame of reference for this thesis.

[6]Quoted in Petermann (2004: 689).

Appendices

(1) JOHN DEENEY, S.J.: A LIFE AMONG THE HO

John Deeney has been described as 'one of the most eminent scholars of the tribal languages of Jharkhand'.[1] Because of his deep immersion into Ho culture for more than half a century his biography is given here. Also, those of his publications which may and will turn out extremely useful for further anthropological research into Ho values and society will be briefly introduced.

Deeney was born in Philadelphia, USA, in 1921. At the age of 18 he joined the Society of Jesus (Jesuits), and the initials 'S.J.' have remained part of his name and identity. He acquired an M.A. in philosophy and went to India in 1949, where he did theological studies and studied Hindi. In 1952 he was ordained a Catholic priest. In the same year he came to Chaibasa, the district capital of Singhbum in the state of Jharkhand. In 1955 he was appointed headmaster of the St. Xavier's High School/ Lupungutu near Chaibasa. He held that position for seven years. He has lived in this region ever since and eventually obtained Indian citizenship in 1991. Even before he became a teacher Deeney had been busy acquiring the Ho language. He made it a point (personal communication) to go by bicycle and see each of his students at their respective homes to become familiar with everyday Ho culture and with his students' background. Whenever he came across a Ho expression that was new to him he would write it down along with the definition and other culturally interesting data on small index cards. He has kept this habit to the present day, and the publication of the Ho-English Dictionary is one of the results.

Deeney is deeply rooted in his Catholic convictions. It is from this source that he has continuously drawn strength. This includes his sincere respect and appreciation of the most divergent expressions of God's creation, and he unconditionally considers the Ho, their language, and their culture as part of this. Deeney has never pretended to be anything but a Jesuit, (a teacher) and a scholar. He is not an anthropologist and has never claimed to be one. Many of his publications are translations into Ho of Catholic prayers, of the New and

[1]D. Prasad in Deeney (2005: back cover).

Old Testament, of Bible readings for the Catholic Mass, and instructions aiming at integrating Ho Christians in a way that pays respect to their indigenous background. His approach is humanistic and not at all patronizing.

Deeney's knowledge of the Ho language has eventually resulted in three publications: a *Ho Grammar and Vocabulary*, a *Ho-English Dictionary* and *An Introduction to the Ho Language*. The first contains a list of kinship terminology, a diagram of the relations of men and women, data on 132 Ho clans or *kilis* (Deeney 2002: 129-32, 135-46)[2] and an English-Ho vocabulary. The second edition of the *Ho-English Dictionary* lists 900 more expressions than the first, with 12,000 entries altogether, and the *Introduction to the Ho Language* has in many cases proved to be a speedy and efficient guide into the first steps of acquiring Ho. These books will prove tremendously insightful for future anthropological research, since they reflect a combined study of Ho language and culture well beyond isolated grammar technicalities and vocabulary denotations. Many examples from and references to the most divergent walks of Ho life and mythology illustrate a world expressed entirely through the eyes of a Ho. Instead of introducing a new script, Deeney makes use of a slightly modified Devanagari. So some basic knowledge of Hindi grammar and spelling is necessary to work through the books, but not Sanskrit.[3]

When Deeney came to India, he had in his baggage a thorough knowledge of English, Latin, Greek, French, and Gaelic grammar. He characterizes Ho as a highly developed language, highly logical and completely regular. This is what he has to say on Ho in his *Ho Grammar and Vocabulary:*

Those who gain facility in understanding Ho will find the language a surprisingly apt instrument for expressing succinctly delicate shades of meaning and . . . subtle turns of thought. . . . When I approach the Ho people from a linguistic view point, observing the capacity of their language for exact expression as well as the rich poetic content of its songs and prayers, I do not feel that the Ho are in any way a primitive people. The richness of the language has given me an added insight

[2]In the first edition of 1975, 124 clans or *kilis* were listed.

[3]For a discussion of a distinctive Ho script as well as problems arising when applying the Devanagari script to a language otherwise not related to the Indo–European Sanskrit, cf. Deeney 2002: xi.

into the deep culture of a people with very delicate refined feelings and sound common sense. . . .

Ironically but understandably the worst Ho is spoken by the most educated . . . [their grammar and vocabulary] heavily influenced by Hindi, and the resulting hodge-podge lacks the richness and clarity of the Ho language as spoken by uneducated men and especially women. (Deeney 2002: ix)

DHANUR SINGH PURTY

Dhanur Singh Purty, a Ho and a graduate of village Karlajuri, has been Deeney's assistant[4] for more than forty years by now. All books published in Ho by Xavier Ho Publications have been written in close collaboration and consultation, every Ho term checked by Purty. During Deeney's time as headmaster, Purty was able to assist an anthropologist who spent two weeks at St. Xavier's High school in Lupungutu/ Chaibasa, interviewing elderly Ho on Ho customs (personal communication). That way he learned about interviewing and tape-recording techniques and modes of transcription.[5] After that, in 1960, Purty began writing on Ho village life and customs himself, and he began by interviewing his father. Between 1978 and 1982 seven books of altogether 1342 pages were written and published in the Ho language. These books have not been translated into English. The Ho-English Dictionary, though, contains all the words used in the seven books.

(2) *HO-DISUM HO HONKO* OR THE HO OF THE HO COUNTRY

This is the title of the seven book series written by Purty in collaboration with Deeney, to which Yorke contributed the photos. Each book carries an individual title reflecting the chosen topics of Ho village life and customs. As they contain informed inside knowledge of Ho culture, a translation of the subject matter of each book is given, plus the headings and sometimes also sub-headings of each chapter, thus providing a rough grid or first overview of the contents for future research on the Ho (incomplete).[6]

[4]Deeney calls him his *pandit*.

[5]Deeney (3/unpubl.: 1).

[6]The translation has been done with the help of my Santal assistant, with the Ho–English Dictionary, and by myself.

CUSTOMS AT THE TIME OF BIRTH, MARRIAGE AND DEATH (BOOK 1)

Chapter 1: *Jonom* or Birth Related Rituals

1. *Hon hobayanre*: after delivery[7]
   - *owa: tameteya*: 'hitting' the house (i.e. breaking the news to the neighbours)
   - *buti lai had*: cutting the umbilical cord
   - *tuka topa*: burying the placenta
   - *guyu*: a temporary hut providing shade
2. *Bisi: chi peyaeyakankin*: social uncleanness or becoming socially defiled, e.g. by child birth
3. *Niyar-ed:* purification rites (shaving); *niyar-era*: 'purification ritual held three days after the birth of a baby after which other people may enter the room where the new mother lives and touch the baby, but the mother and whoever shares the social impurity with her may not yet enter the family *adin* nor touch the family *mandi chatu* until the final purification (*tiki-era*) has taken place' (Deeney 2005: 267).
4. *Tiki-ed:* 3. ctd, to boil (clothes) in water. *Tiki-era*: 'the final purification ceremony about 30 days after childbirth' (ibid.: 380).
5. *Nutum tupu-nam*: searching for a name; literally: to find out by dipping ('used of the process of selecting a name for a baby by placing *ramba*, i.e. a green gram or cultivated pulse, seeds . . . in a lot of water and watching whether or not the seeds come together') (ibid.: 395).
6. *Nutum sapaki:* ritual of finding a namesake
   - Feast to be given by the parents of the babies
   - Relatives to be informed
   - Chicken or goat to be offered
   - String on baby (*dora*)

Chapter 2: *Gonoe*: or Death Related Rituals

1. *Topa*: burying (as opposed to 'cremating', see below)
2. *Hasa huwan*: the grave
3. *Tapangi*: waiting for one another
4. *Hasa-huwante goe:yakan ho aḍer*: burying the body in the grave
5. *Til diyan*: 'rice beer intended for presentation, used e.g. of 1) rice beer brought to the house where a person has died to be given to

[7]Literally: when the child is ready.

the family and those who help and attend the burial. . . ' (ibid.: 381)

6. *Keya-aderi dinili*: fixing a date for calling the shade of someone dead inside the *adin*
7. *Karkad emeteya: ondo: moda odakon chelan*: offering a toothstick and water to the soul of the dead
8. *Keya-ader*: calling the soul into the *adin*
9. *rapa*: : cremating a body
10. *diri or-topa ondo: dul sunum reya: jom-nu*: setting the burial stone, pouring oil on it, celebrating (i.e. eating, drinking) together
11. *jan topa*: burying the bones of a dead person whose body has been cremated. 'This burial is done with ceremony usually after some delay, sometimes as long as a year after the death' (ibid.: 172).

FESTIVALS OR POROBKO (BOOK 2)

The chapters of this book follow the yearly cycle of the principal Ho feasts.

1. *Mage porob:* 'feast observed in each village after the harvest work is finished; obscene language used then' (Deeney 2005: 240).[8]
2. *Ba porob:* 'annual flower feast celebrated when the white flowers of the sal or *sarjom* tree blossom' (ibid.: 20).[9]
3. *Baba or Her mut/mutu:* 'sacrifice and feast held before the sowing of the main paddy crop' (ibid.: 150).
4. *Hero porob:* 'the sacrifice and feast held after all the sowing has been completed about the month of July' (ibid.).
5. *Batauli:* 'feast to obtain proper rain, a sacrifice to obtain protection for the paddy' (ibid.: 34).
6. *Jom nama porob:* 'feast celebrated when the harvesting of the upland crop is started before the first fruits of the harvest are eaten' (ibid.: 184).
7. *Hiyad-murgad*: 'a sacrifice performed at the time of or after the *jom nama* feast' (ibid.: 154).
8. *Kolomreya: dosturko* or *kolom utari*: 'prayers and chicken sacrifices performed on the threshing floor after all the work of

[8]In Manbir, *mage porob* was celebrated in February 2006 beginning a fortnight before full moon, the main day of the festival falling exactly on the full moon day.

[9]*Ba porob* in Manbir was celebrated on the full moon day of March 2006.

the threshing and bringing in the paddy has been completed. This is offered in thanksgiving, and to rectify any offences which may have been made to the spirits (especially to *baba enga*) during the process of threshing' (ibid.: 209).

9. *Gau mara*: 'a feast held in some villages at which rice beer is given to cow-herders' (ibid.: 120).
(*Owa: di or owa: andi:* a ritual celebrated on the occasion of a new house).

HOSPITALITY, ACTIVITIES, AND ATTITUDES (BOOK 3)

This book is a collection of nine essays on various topics.

1. *kupul em-ched* or hospitality towards a guest. This essay is about how visiting guests are received in a Ho house.[10]
2. *man-mapan is* a generic term for respect relationships.

3-5. *ote-taso*: cultivating fields; *kolom paiti*: working on the threshing ground; *bandi ader*: pulling the rice bundle inside. In three essays the work cycle of the main paddy crop from the first ploughing to the storing of the harvest in the house is described.

6. *lungam anda* or 'a place for silkworms' is an essay on silkworm breeding.
7. *dongol hato:* (old) Chaibasa market. This essay is also about the social quality of marketplaces in the life of a Ho.
8. *hoyo-gama ondo: sumuki- ringareya: chinako*: rain and wind related to signs of abundance. An essay on how the Ho 'read' and predict weather.
9. *hasuko ondo: red-ranuko*: illnesses and medicines.

FROM INFANCY TO OLD AGE (BOOK 5)[11]

1. *Honko*: children
2. *Sepedeyan-hapanumeyanre*: about young men and young girls (a chapter on adolescence)
3. *Eran ondo*: *howanre*: about wife and husband, man and woman
4. *Hameyan-buriyanre*: about old men and women.

[10]The short information on each chapter follows the foreword to the third book.

[11]Unfortunately Book (4) on *Singbonga and the Bongas* was out of print and not available to me.

According to Deeney this is the best of the seven books, providing a panoramic view of Ho life.[12]

HUNTING (BOOK 6)

This book covers the whole range from big game hunting in thick jungle to catching flying ants. Deeney claims that to really know a Ho it is essential to know about the hunting dimension of his life.[13]

A chapter on a cock fight is added, since a 'defeated cock is treated with the same respect and taboos with which an animal killed in a hunt would be treated' (Deeney [in Purty1981]: foreword).

1. *Buru sangar:* hunting in the jungle
2. *Sangil sangar:* hunting a bison
3. *Sangarreya: neled-med kajiko*: hunting tales
4. *Kulae sangar:* hunting rabbits or hares
5. *Jiki sangar:* hunting porcupines
6. *Oe sangar:* hunting birds
7. *Hakuko sab:* catching fish
8. *Burdud sab:* catching flying ants: 'the winged female of white ants which swarm out of ant-hills of the earth esp. at the beginning of the monsoon' Deeney (2005: 54)
9. *Sim tol:* (a) tying a sharp blade to the natural spur of a cock for fight; (b) entering a cock into a cockfight (ibid.: 386)

[12]There are too many subchapters to be translated within the scope of this paper.

[13]This coincides with what Deeney said when we discussed the outspokenness and self-confidence that Ho women conveyed to me (personal communication). Ho men's pride and self-esteem, Deeney claimed, depended greatly on their hunting success, their ability to use bow-and-arrow. In his view the lack of huntable animals in the deforested jungle now poses a serious threat to male Ho identity. Hunting and shooting the arrow link a Ho to the sphere of the divine and go well beyond providing meat for a meal. On the occasion of *ba porob*, the flower or spring festival, a big branch of a sal tree or *sarjom daru* is cut and put inside the sacred grove or *desauli*. A ritual or *bonga* addressed to the village guardian spirit is performed at the foot of the branch, before it is taken outside the stone circle surrounding the *desauli*. It is fixed upright in the ground serving as the target to be hit in the shooting competition from a distance of some fifty metres. In Pathan Sai, the village of my namesake or *saki*, the competition was carried through when it was so dark that I could not see the branch any more.

MYTHS AND OLD STORIES (BOOK 7)

The last of the seven books contains old myths of origin, the Asur legend, stories, proverbs, folk sayings, riddles and their solutions. To convey a rather representative picture of what is alive in Ho awareness, Ho people of older and young generations have been contacted, invited to contribute, and tape recorded.

(3) *MIYAD MANDI CHATURENKO* OR PEOPLE OF ONE RICE POT

ANCESTORS OF CHUMBURU PURTY, *MUNDA* OR VILLAGE HEADMAN FROM PATHAN SAI, TARANA, MAYURBHANJ, ORISSA, INDIA.

This illustration of *miyad mandi chaturenko* refers to Chapters One and Five. It contains 'all those descended from a common ancestor, from people who once ate from the same rice pot' (Deeney 2005: 242), alive and dead. Those who have died represent the ancestors to be named in rituals or *bongas*. Here our namesakes' or *sakis*' ancestors or *ham hoko* are given. Their names will be called out – from left to right, from top to bottom – in the course of rituals in all the households of those so related, an affair well beyond the village level.

Some necessary explanations concerning the illustration:

- All *bongas* being with Manai Purty (0) of the (+4) generational level. After that all the other names will be called out. Manai Purty was from Kati Gutu near Chaibasa.
- Sorgod (1) and his branch of the Halong Purty *kili* migrated to Cuttak from there.
- Manai (2) had two wives and eleven sons, but the names of only three sons were given to me.
- Kirsai (3), Chumburu Purty's (7) FFF or great grandfather, settled in Pathan Sai.
- Randor (4) migrated to Rasika Sai.
- Our *sakis* are Chumburu Purty (7) of the Halong Purty *kili* and his wife (6).
- Uma Kanto of the (-1) generational level, was our *sakis*' only son. As he is dead, he is the last of the 26 ancestors to be mentioned in the bongas.
- Ancestors: male ▲ and female ●
- △ = male (alive) ○ = female (alive)

Bibliography

Bachmann, Ingeborg 2005[1978]. *Sämtliche Gedichte*, München: Serie Pieper.

Bailey, Frederick G. 1960. *Tribe, Caste and Nation: A Study of Political Activity and Political Change in Highland Orissa*, Manchester: Manchester University Press.

——— 1961. '"Tribe" and "Caste" in India', *Contributions to Indian Sociology*, vol. V, pp. 6–19.

Bauer, Eva Maria 1987 (unpublished). 'Die sozialen Institutionen der Ho im Singhbum-Distrikt des indischen Bundesstaates Bihar'. Magisterarbeit an der Fakultät für Orientalistik und Altertumswissenschaft. Fachbereich Ethnologie, Heidelberg.

Berger, Peter 2007. *Füttern, Speisen und Verschlingen: Ritual und Gesellschaft im Hochland von Orissa, Indien*, Berlin: Lit Verlag.

——— 1999. 'Von Häusern und Gräbern. Über die Bestattungsrituale der Toraja auf Sulawesi, Indonesien', in *Die lange Reise der Toten. Zwei Studien zu Ideologie und Praxis des Todes in Süd- und Südostasien.* Wissenschaftliche Schriften zur Ethnologie und Anthropologie. Schriftenreihe Herodot, Bd. 3, Hamburg: Verlag Dr. Kovac, 5–162.

Berger, Peter and R. Kottmann 2000. *Die lange Reise der Toten. Zwei Studien zu Ideologie und Praxis des Todes in Süd- und Südostasien*, Hamburg: Kovac.

Bloch, Maurice and Jonathan P. Parry 1982. 'Introduction: Death and the Regeneration of Life', in *Death and the Regeneration of Life*. Cambridge: Cambridge University Press, pp. 1–44.

Bloch, Maurice 1988. 'Introduction: Death and the Concept of a Person', in *On the Meaning of Death: Essays on Mortuary Rituals and Eschatological Beliefs*, ed. S. Cederroth, C. Corlin and J. Lindström, Uppsala, pp. 11–30.

Boas, Franz 1911. *The Mind of Primitive Man*, New York: MacMillan.

Cederroth, Sven, Claes Corlin and Jan Lindström, 1988 (eds.). *On the Meaning of Death: Essays on Mortuary Rituals and Eschatological Beliefs*. Introduction by Maurice Bloch, Uppsala.

Census of India 1991. India at a Glance: Scheduled Castes and Scheduled Tribes http://www.censusindia.net/scst.html. 22.07.2007.

——— 2001. T 00-005: Total Population of Scheduled Castes and Scheduled Tribes and their Proportions to the Total Population. Primary Census Abstract. http://www.censusindia.net/t_00_005.html. 22.07.2007.

——— 2001. Jharkhand: Data Highlights: The Scheduled Tribes, Office of the Registrar General, India.

Census of Orissa 2001. Cf. www.orissagov.nic.in/census.(23.06.2007)

Clark, Brian 1978 [1972]. *Whose Life is it Anyway*? Ashover, Derbvshire: Amber Lane Productions Ltd.

Coppet, Daniel de 1981. 'The Life-Giving Death', in *Mortality and Immortality: The Anthropology and Archaeology of Death*, ed. S.C. Humphreys and H. King, London: Academic Press, pp. 175–204.

Dhan, Rekha O. 1961. 'The Hos of Saranda: An Ethnographic Study', *Bulletin of the Bihar Tribal Research Centre,* vol. III, no. 1, Ranchi: The Bihar Tribal Research Institute, pp. 37–114.

Dhan, Rekha O. 1962. 'The Religion of the Hos of Saranda', in *Bulletin of the Bihar Tribal Research Centre,* vol. IV, no. 1, Ranchi: The Bihar Tribal Research Institute, pp. 17–35.

Deeney, John, 2005[1978]. *Ho-English Dictionary*, new edn, revised and enlarged, Ranchi: Xavier Publications, Catholic Press.

——— 2002 [1975]. *Ho Grammar and Vocabulary*, 2nd edn., Chaibasa: Xavier Ho Publications.

——— 1991. *Introduction to the Ho Language*, Chaibasa: Xavier Ho Publications.

——— 2008. *The Spirit World of the Ho Tribals. And other Glimpses into the Ho World*, Ranchi: Xavier Publications.

——— (1/unpubl.). 'The Husband in the Role of the Midwife: A Custom of the Ho Tribe'.

——— (2/unpubl.). 'The Hos' Continued Relationship with their Dead'.

——— (3/unpubl.). 'The Spirit World of the Ho as Seen from a Christian Perspective'.

——— (n.d.). 'Some Theological Reflections on Ancestor Veneration Among the Hos'. *Sevartham.*

Demmer, Ulrich 2007. 'Memory, Performance and the Regeneration of Society Among the Koya', in *Time in India: Concepts and Practices.* ed. Angelika Malinar, vol. 6, pp. 185–201, Delhi: Manohar.

Dumont, Louis 1961. 'Caste, Racism, and "Stratification": Reflections of a Social Anthropologist', *Contributions to Indian Sociology.* vol. V, pp. 20–43.

——— 1962. 'Correspondence: "Tribe" and "Caste" in India', *Contributions to Indian Sociology*, vol. VI, pp. 120–2.

——— 1970 [1966]. *Homo Hierarchicus: The Caste System and its Implications,* London: Weidenfeld and Nicolson.

——— 1986. *Essays on Individualism: Modern Ideology in Anthropological Perspective*, Chicago: The University of Chicago Press.

Elwin, Verrier 1939. *The Baiga*, London: John Murray.

——— 1947. *The Murja and their Ghotul,* Bombay: Oxford University Press.

——— 1955. *The Religion of an Indian Tribe*, Bombay: Oxford University Press.

Evans-Pritchard, Edward E. 1960. Introduction, in Robert Hertz, 1960 [1907 in French]. 'A Contribution to the Study of the Collective Representation of Death', in *Death and the Right Hand*, translated by Rodney and Claudia Needham, Aberdeen: Cohen & West, 9–24.

Fabian, Johannes 1973. 'How Others Die: Reflections on the Anthropology of Death', in *Death in American Experience*, ed. Arien Mack, New York: Schocken, pp. 177–201.

Frazer, James 1890. *The Golden Bough: A Study in Comparative Religion*, London.

Fried, Morton H. 1966. 'On the Concepts of "Tribe" and "Tribal Society"', in *Transactions of the New York Academy of Science*, Ser. 2, vol. 28, pp. 527–40.

Fuerer-Haimendorf, Christoph von 1950. 'Youth Dormitories and Community Houses in India: 'A Restatement and Review', in *Anthropos* 45: 119–144.

Gell, Simeran Man Singh 1992. *The Ghotul in Muria Society,* Chur: Harwood Academic Publishers.

Gluckman, Max 1960. 'Tribalism in Modern British Central Africa', in *Cahiers d'études africaines* 1. 55–70.

Hardenberg, Roland Josef 2005 (Habilitation thesis, unpubl.). 'Children of the Earth Goddess: Society, Marriage and Sacrifice in the Highlands of Orissa', Münster.

Helander, Berhard 1988. 'Death and the End of Society: Official Ideology and Ritual Communication in the Somali Funeral', in Sven Cederroth, Claes Corlin and Jan Lindström 1988 (eds.). *On the Meaning of Death. Essays on Mortuary Rituals and Eschatological Beliefs*, Introduction by Maurice Bloch, Uppsala.

Hertz, Robert 1960 [1907 in French]. 'A Contribution to the Study of the Collective Representation of Death', in *Death and the Right Hand*, tr. Rodney Needham and Claudia Needham, with an Introduction by E.E. Evans-Pritchard, Aberdeen: Cohen & West, pp. 27-86.

Hoffmann, John and Arthur van Emelen 1990 [1950]. *Encyclopedia Mundarica*, New Delhi.

Hornby, A.S. 1995. *Oxford Advanced Learner's Dictionary of Current English*, 5th edn., Oxford: Oxford University Press.

Humphreys, Sally C. and Helen King 1981 (eds.), *Mortality and Immortality: The Anthropology and Archaeology of Death*, London: Academic Press.

Humphreys, Sally C. 1980. 'Death and Time', in 1981 (eds.), *Mortality and Immortality: The Anthropology and Archaeology of Death*, ed. S.C. Humphreys and H. King, London: Academic Press, pp. 261–83.

Huntington, Richard and Peter Metcalf 1979. *Celebrations of Death: The Anthropology of Mortuary Ritual*, Cambridge: Cambridge University Press.

Kottmann, Rainer 1999. Tod in der Sora-Gesellschaft. 'Dialoge mit den Toten'. Die Feldforschung von Vitebsky bei einer mittelindischen Ethnie, in 2000. *Die lange Reise der Toten: Zwei Studien zu Ideologie und Praxis des Todes in Süd- und Südostasien*, ed. Peter Berger and Rainer Kottmann, Hamburg: Schriftenreihe Herodot, Bd. 3, 167–305.

Kuper, Adam 1988. *The Invention of Primitive Society: Transformations of an Illusion,* London: Routledge.

Leach, Edmund R. 1977 [1954]. *Political Systems of Highland Burma: A Study of Kachin Social Structure*, London: Athlone.

——— 1958. 'Magical Hair', *The Journal of the Royal Anthropological Institute,* 88, pp. 147–64.

Lévi-Strauss, Claude 1970[1955]. *Traurige Tropen. Indianer in Brasilien*, Köln: Kiepenheuer & Witsch.

Majumdar, D.N. 1950. *The Affairs of a Tribe: A Study in Tribal Dynamics*, Lucknow: Universal Publishers.

McDougal, Charles Walter 1963. 'The Social Structure of the Hill Juang'. Dissertation submitted to the University of New Mexico.

Needham, Rodney 1981. 'Inner States as Universals: Sceptical Reflections on Human Nature', in *Indigenous Psychologies: The Anthropology of the Self*, ed. P. Heelas and A. Lock, London: Academic Press, pp. 65–78.

Otten, Tina 2006. *Heilung durch Rituale. Vom Umgang mit Krankheit bei den Rona im Hochland Orissas.* Indus. Ethnologische Südasien-Studien, Bd. 9, Berlin: Lit Verlag.

Parry, Jonathan 1986. 'Death and Digestion: The Symbolism of Food and Eating in North Indian Mortuary Rites', in *Man (N.S.)*, 20, pp. 612–30.

Petermann, Werner 2004. *Die Geschichte der Ethnologie.* Edition Trickster, Wuppertal: Peter Hammer Verlag.

Pfeffer, Georg 1994. 'Die kulturelle Verarbeitung des Todes', in *Mitteilungen der Berliner Gesellschaft für Anthropologie, Ethnologie und Urgeschichte.* 15, 9–13.

——— 1996. 'The Young and the Junior Set in Tribal Middle India', in *Contemporary Society: Childhood and Complex Order*, ed. G. Pfeffer and D.K. Behera, Delhi: Manak, pp. 98–109.

——— 1997. 'The Scheduled Tribes of Middle India as a Unit: Problems of Internal and External Comparison', in *Contemporary Society: Tribal Studies*, vol. I: *Structure and Process*, ed. G. Pfeffer and D.K. Behera, Delhi: Concept, pp. 3–27.

——— 2000a. 'Tribal Ideas', *Journal of Social Sciences (JSS)*, vol. 4, no. 4, Special Issue: *Asian World Views: Context and Structure*, ed. Roland Hardenberg, pp. 331–46.

——— 2000b. 'Tribal Society of Highland Orissa, Highland Burma, and Elsewhere', in *Text and Context*, ed. A. Malinar, H. Frese, and J. Beltz, Delhi: Manohar, pp. 10–29.

——— 2001. 'A Ritual of Revival Among the Gadaba of Koraput', in *Jagannath Revisited: Studying Society, Religion and the State of Orissa*, ed. H. Kulke and B. Schnepel, Delhi: Manohar, pp. 123–48.

——— 2002a. 'Introduction', in *Contemporary Society: Tribal Studies*, vol. V: *Concept of Tribal Society*, ed. G. Pfeffer and D.K. Behera, Delhi: Concept, pp. 9–28.

——— 2002b. 'The Structure of Middle Indian Tribal Society Compared', in *Contemporary Society: Tribal Studies*, vol. V, *Concept of Tribal Society*, ed. G. Pfeffer and D.K. Behera, Delhi: Concept, pp. 208–29.

——— 2002c. (unpubl. manuscript). 'Debating the Tribe', Heidelberg: European Conference on Modern South Asian Studies.

——— 2002d. *Hunters, Tribes, Peasants: Cultural Crisis and Comparison: The Dr. Ambedkar Memorial Lecture Series*, Orissa: National Institute of Social Work and Social Sciences.

——— (unpubl.). 'Sahlins' Tribesmen Reconsidered: Highland Orissa in Eastern India'.

Purty, Dhanur Singh 1978–82. *Ho-Disum Ho Honko. A Series of 7 Books in Ho Language*, Chaibasa: Xavier Ho Publications.

Redfield , Robert 1947. 'Folk Society', in *American Journal of Sociology* 52, 293–308.

Robben, Antonius C.G.M. (ed.) 2004. *Death, Mourning, and Burial: A Cross-Cultural Reader*, Massachusetts: Blackwell Publishing.

Rosaldo, Renato 1993[1989]. 'Introduction: Grief and a Headhunter's Rage', in *Culture and Truth: The Remaking of Social Analysis.* Boston: Beacon Press, pp. 1–21.

Roy, Sarat C. 1925. *The Birhors: A Little Known Jungle Tribe of Chota Nagpur,* Ranchi: The G.E.L. Mission Press.

——— 1937. *The Kharias,* 2 vols., Ranchi: 'Man in India' Office.

Said, Edward W. 1995 [1978]. *Orientalism: Western Conceptions of the Orient,* New Delhi: Penguin Books.

Sahlins, Marshall D. 1968. *Tribesmen,* Foundations of Modern Anthropology Series, Englewood Cliffs: Prentice-Hall.

Scheper-Hughes, Nancy 1992. *Death Without Weeping: The Violence of Everyday Life in Brazil,* Berkeley: University of California Press.

Skoda, Uwe 2004. 'Adivasi'. http://www.südasien.info/laenderinfos/462. 2.02.2007.

——— 2005. *The Aghria: A Peasant Caste on a Tribal Frontier*, Delhi: Manohar.

Southall, Aidan W. 1970. 'The Illusion of the Tribe', in Peter W. Gutkind (ed.), *The Passing of Tribal Man in Africa*, Leiden: Brill, pp. 28–50.

Trawick, Margaret 1992[1990]. *Notes on Love in a Tamil Family*, Berkeley: University of California Press.

Van Gennep, Arnold 1960[1909]. *The Rites of Passage*, London: Routledge.

Vitebsky, Piers 1993. *Dialogues with the Dead: The Discussion of Mortality Among the Sora of Eastern India,* Cambridge: Cambridge University Press.

Yorke, Michael P. 1976 (unpubl.). 'Decisions and Analogy: Political Structure and Discourse Among the Ho Tribals of India', Ph.D. thesis submitted to the School of Oriental and African Studies, University of London.

Zimpel, Heinz-Gerhard and Walter de Gruyler 2001. *Lexikon der Weltbevölkerung. Geographie- Kultur- Gesellschaft,* Berlin, New York.

Index